CASCADIA
GARDENING
SERIES

North Coast Roses

For the Maritime Northwest Gardener

Rhonda Massingham Hart

Sasquatch Books
Seattle

To my husband, Lance — A perfect rose, thorns and all.

Thanks to the helpful rose gardeners from British Columbia, Washington, Oregon, northern California, and beyond—many of whom the reader will meet in this book. And special thanks to Wendy Turner and Scott Johns for being there!

Printed in the United States of America

Cover design: Kris Morgan Design
Cover photograph: 'Headliner', a tall Hybrid Tea bush, registered in 1985.
   Photograph by David McDonald.
Interior design: Lynne Faulk Design
Interior illustrations: Celeste Henriquez. Illustration on page 50 adapted with permission from *Without a Thorn*, by Stuart Mechlin and Ellen Bonanno, published 1978 by Timber Press.
Composition: Scribe Typography
Photographs in color insert: John Frost: p.2, bottom; p.6, bottom left; p.7, bottom left and right. Bob Gold: p.5, top. Daniel Hinkley: p.1, bottom left; p.8, bottom left. David McDonald: p.6, top left and right, bottom right; p.8, bottom right. Margaret Mulligan: p.1, bottom right. Don Normark: p.2, top left; p.3, top. Joy Spurr: p.2, top right; p.3, bottom. Linda Younker: p.1, top; p.4; p.5, bottom; p.7, top; p.8, top.

Library of Congress Cataloging in Publication Data
Hart, Rhonda Massingham, 1959–
    North coast roses : for the maritime Northwest gardener / Rhonda Massingham Hart.
        p. cm. — (Cascadia gardening series)
    Includes bibliographical references (p.) and index.
    ISBN 0-912365-76-5 : $8.95
    1. Rose culture — Northwest Coast of North America. 2. Roses — Northwest Coast of North America. I. Title. II. Series.
    SB411.H335 1993
    635.9'33372'09795 — dc20   92-42243
                                                                 CIP

Published by Sasquatch Books
1931 Second Avenue, Seattle, Washington 98101, (206) 441-6202

Other titles in the Cascadia Gardening Series:
Water-Wise Vegetables, by Steve Solomon
Winter Ornamentals, by Daniel Hinkley (forthcoming)
The Herb-Gardener's Handbook, by Mary Preus (forthcoming)

Contents

Classification Codes

The following American Rose Society abbreviations are used in this book to designate rose colors, classifications, and types.

COLORS

ab	apricot blend	**my**	medium yellow
dp	deep pink	**op**	orange-pink
dr	dark red	**or**	orange-red
dy	deep yellow	**ob**	orange and orange blend
lp	light pink	**pb**	pink blend
ly	light yellow	**rb**	red blend
m	mauve and mauve blend	**yb**	yellow blend
mp	medium pink	**w**	white, near white, and
mr	medium red		white blend

CLASSIFICATIONS AND TYPES

A	Alba	**HRg**	Hybrid Rugosa
B	Bourbon	**HSpn**	Hybrid Spinosissima
C	Centifolia	**HT**	Hybrid Tea
Ch	China	**K**	Kordesii
Cl	Climber	**LCl**	Large-Flowered Climber
ClB	Climbing Bourbon	**M**	Moss
ClMin	Climbing Miniature	**Min**	Miniature
ClT	Climbing Tea	**N**	Noisette
D	Damask	**OGR**	Old Garden Roses
F	Floribunda	**P**	Portland
G	Gallica	**R**	Rambler
Gr	Grandiflora	**Pol**	Polyantha
HBc	Hybrid Bracteata	**S**	Shrub
HMoy	Hybrid Moyesii	**Sp**	Species
HMsk	Hybrid Musk	**T**	Tea
HP	Hybrid Perpetual		

Gardening in the Maritime Northwest

The maritime Northwest—lying west of the Cascade Range and running from British Columbia to northern California—is often called Cascadia. With its warm dry summers and cool rainy winters, this region offers particular challenges to regional gardeners. In addition to its temperate but often unpredictable weather, Cascadia is characterized by glacial soils, dramatic topography, and a growing population that is straining water supplies in urban areas. It is also a land blessed with both a full spectrum of native flora and ideal growing conditions for a vast array of non-native plants.

The Cascadia Gardening Series addresses the challenges and benefits of gardening in the maritime Northwest. Topics in the series cover both ornamental and food crops, and provide experienced as well as novice gardeners with up-to-date information and advice. The series authors rely on local knowledge, personal experience, and the counsel of regional gardening experts. Cultivation data is adapted to regional microclimates and soils, and recommendations for maintaining a healthy garden are tailored to specific conditions. Each book includes suggestions for drought- and pest-resistance varieties, landscaping, irrigation techniques, and plant selection.

The goal of the series is to help gardeners increase their knowledge, understanding, and enjoyment of gardening in the maritime Northwest. Please let us know what you think of this book, and what topics you would like to see explored in upcoming books in the Cascadia Gardening Series.

Cascadia Gardening Series
Sasquatch Books
1931 Second Avenue
Seattle, WA 98101

—*The Editors*

The Incomparable Rose

My earliest memories of roses are of two large mounds that grew in front of the old house on the family homestead. Late every spring those immense briars would erupt into a medley of beauty, fragrance, and sound. Yes, sound. You couldn't go near them during the daylight hours without a constant serenade from hundreds of happy bees. Sadly, however, the bushes would finish their blooming within weeks. I always wondered what was "wrong" with them, why they didn't bloom all summer like my mother's did. But these were roses of another generation, planted by my grandmother when she was a young bride. Though I never have figured out precisely what variety they were, they planted a seed that grows to this day—my love of roses.

I wrote this book to disclose the secrets I've learned about growing roses in the maritime Northwest. Though much of the area offers nearly ideal growing conditions for most types of roses, there are strategies to ensure your success—even in challenging locations. You'll learn the crucial preliminaries of selecting the best varieties for your garden and preparing the soil bed, as well as the basics of site selection, feeding, watering, and pruning.

North Coast Roses also will help you figure out how to put all this information to work in your own circumstances. For instance, if you're like me and don't have a lot of time to spend tending roses, I will recommend that you grow primarily kill-proof types, such as 'Königin von Dänemark', 'The Fairy', and various rugosa roses. If you have more time, there are roses you can pamper for beautiful rewards.

As I visited rose gardens and interviewed diverse people for this book, it became very clear to me that roses are a great common denominator. People who you might not think would have much to say to each other opened up instantly when asked about their roses. Everyone, it seems, has an opinion! Boxed lists throughout the book will show you at a glance some of the favorites of the rose enthusiasts I interviewed.

Of course, each individual's preference in roses is very subjective. Personal choice and style help determine which roses you prefer, as do the inevitable differences in your growing site. The maritime Northwest boasts a variety of micro-environments, each presenting its own unique challenges. This book will explain how to deal with them to grow beautiful roses.

I invite you to share what I've learned during a lifetime of rose growing throughout the north Pacific coast, and from taking the generous advice of experts whose common bond is raising these incomparable flowers.

—Rhonda Massingham Hart

Note: Throughout this book I have used the following terms for designating flower forms:

Single roses have 5 to 8 petals.

Semi-double roses have 8 to 20 petals in up to three rows.

Double roses have 25 or more petals.

Very double have between 35 and 40 to 100 or more petals.

Best North Coast Roses

CHAPTER 1

FROM EURASIA TO THE NORTHWEST

People have enjoyed roses since long before recorded history. Varieties native to the Orient and Europe have been cultivated since the 12th century B.C. As travel and trade began to expand, these roses were finally introduced to each other in the early 1800s. The first hybrids were the result of natural cross-pollination, but eventually the process became more sophisticated as humans discovered more direct ways to intervene.

About 2,000 individual species of roses are described and named worldwide. The varieties and hybrids of these species expand the list of known roses to well over 20,000, with more added to the list each year.

CHOOSING FOR YOUR GARDEN

With so many types of roses and varieties available to the North Coast gardener, how do you choose the right ones for your landscape? First, consider the individual traits of each type of rose, such as the spreading tendencies of older varieties or their limited flowering time. Then consider the space you have and the nature of the site. Some rose types demand less space than others and a few will even tolerate shade. Presented here are the best roses for the north Pacific coast. The list offers something for you, whatever your growing conditions.

Species Roses

Wild roses had claimed every continent in the northern hemisphere long before anyone was around to stop and smell them. Each species, separated geographically from the others, developed its unique characteristics. Many are still available and are popular for being easy to care for, as well as pretty.

Rosa gallica. With its deep pink blossoms, this is one of the most cherished species in the region. The species *gallica* is accepted to be the common ancestor of the Old Garden Roses, many of which are the forerunners of today's Hybrid Tea and Shrub Roses.

Rosa nutkana. When choosing a rose to suit the north Pacific coast, what could be more natural than the native Nootka Rose? This wilding is a fine choice for a tall, spreading hedge. Masses of them thrive along Interstate 5 to cushion the roadside view. Though the fragrance of an individual blossom is slight, a hedge in full bloom releases a potent perfume. Once the blossoms fade and begin to fall, bright orange hips and red stems carry the show into winter. It is disease free, hearty, and reliable.

Rosa woodsii. This North American native also prospers in the region. It, too, can be found along sections of I-5, a testament to its self-sufficiency. The bush grows to over 5 feet tall and spreads as wide. In early summer, small clusters of medium pink, single blossoms appear. They are followed by clusters of showy orange hips.

Rosa gymnocarpa. The Woods Rose, another North American native, also was incorporated into many I-5 plantings. The bush grows to only about 2½ feet tall. The light pink, single blossoms are likewise very petite and the hips that follow correspondingly small. Though not a particularly spectacular specimen, it is one of the few roses that will tolerate wet soil.

Rosa glauca. Fast becoming a favorite of Northwest horticulturists, this rose is described by Charles Price of the landscape design firm Withey-Price in aptly poetic terms: "If left unpruned, it will grow into a large arching shrub with leaden, steely blue-green leaves that appear more blue in shade, more mauve in sunlight, with stems that run to dark damson purple in winter." The unusual foliage makes it desirable as a landscape plant, as does its drought tolerance.

Rosa nitida. This North American native is favored for its remarkable foliage. The shiny leaves showcase single pink flowers in early summer, soon to be followed by dark red hips; in the fall they take on a deep maroon color. This species grows in bogs and marshes, so it provides an excellent solution for the problem of wet soils.

Rosa × paulii. Sometimes it is not so much beauty that attracts us to a rose as its sheer usefulness. *Rosa × paulii* has both. It sprawls out to cover an area 10 feet or more across. The vigorous growth stays low to the ground and fills in with attractive foliage—all of which makes a truly effective ground cover. In the early summer this blanket of green explodes into bloom with a mass of pure white, single blossoms that resemble those of clematis. The fall foliage takes on bright hues of yellow and orange to further complement its range of talents. The one drawback to this rose is its innate susceptibility to mildew.

Rosa banksiae. Also known as the Lady Banks rose, this unusual plant makes a lovely addition to any rose collection. Large, full clusters of sweet-smelling blossoms erupt in the late spring in white or soft yellow, depending upon the variety. The petals are small and clustered, as in carnations. The canes of the hardier yellow variety 'Lutea' grow up to 25 feet or more, while the white 'Alba Plena' is more suited to growing in hedgerows. These roses are nearly repellent to aphids and extremely disease resistant, though best in lots of sun.

Rosa eglanteria. If you need to fill in a large area with a robust, hardy, unusual rose, this may be the perfect choice. The European sweetbriar rose has adapted quite well to our climate. It produces long canes that will cover an area 12 feet across or better.

The single, pink blossoms are borne in early summer and are lightly fragrant, but the leaves are what makes the sweetbriar sweet. The scent of fresh-cut apples is magnified after a rain or upon bruising the foliage. "The whole plant is so wonderfully fragrant for three to four months of the year," delights Charles Price. The bright red hips stay well into winter if the birds don't get them first.

Rosa spinosissima (= *R. pimpinellifolia*). Another species doing well for western Washington's highway beautification project is the Scotch Briar rose, remarkable for its toughness and disease resistance. One of the best varieties for home gardeners is the delightful 'Double White', which produces a flood of tiny, scented flowers that last nearly a month, and is disease free.

Rosa multiflora. Though native to Japan and other areas of the Far East, this rose has naturalized here. Canes up to 5 yards long form a thorny mound that presents clusters of small white flowers in early summer. This tough, trouble-free rose thrives in poor soils, making it a popular choice. Although you may never have seen *R. multiflora* in bloom, you have surely witnessed the evidence of its strong roots—it is one of the most commonly used varieties for rootstock on grafted roses.

Rosa foetida. This species has influenced many modern varieties.

Species Favorites

White/White Blend

R. *brunonii* w (also known as
R. *moschata nepalensis* w)
R. *rugosa* 'Alba' w
R. *sericea* var. *omeiensis* forma
pteracantha (red thorns) w
R. *soulieana* w
R. *spinosissima altaica* w

Yellow

R. *banksiae lutea* my

Pink/Pink Blend

Rosa *eglanteria* lp
R. *glauca* mp
R. *nutkana* mp
R. *pomifera* mp
R. *rugosa rubra* mp
R. *woodsii* mp

Mauve/Mauve Blend

R. *rugosa* m

The introduction of the variety 'Persian Yellow' into the line of Hybrid Teas gave Teas their yellow color and near-fatal flaw. Though very hardy and remarkable for the vibrant yellow color it has passed on, R. *foetida* is very prone to blackspot and, sadly, passes this trait along to its descendants. You have to be willing to spray religiously or it may be a poor choice. The sport (mutation) R. *foetida* 'Bicolor', also known as 'Austrian Copper', is among the roses recommended for drought tolerance by plant expert Dan Borroff of Dan Borroff Landscape.

Rosa *rugosa*. If you're interested in easy-to-grow, healthy roses, the Rugosa Rose is a milestone in rose culture. The silken, single mauve blossoms smell like cinnamon or cloves. They may appear individually or in clusters and continue to form as the plant is setting the large, round, orange-and-red hips, which creates a bright fall show. Plants grow upright to 6 feet tall. Given this rose's tolerance of poor soil, neglect, harsh weather, and indifference to disease, it is one of the most important roses for hybridizing a new generation of tough, beautiful varieties.

Rosarians from the seaside to the high foothills concede the universality of Rosa *rugosa*. Scott Stiles of Raintree Nursery, in Morton, Washington, in the Cascade foothills, is a serious proponent of nontoxic gardening who praises the Rugosa Rose as offering the best of both worlds. "If you want a nice-looking, fragrant rose bush that you can grow chemical free, look into Rugosas. They do well just about anywhere."

Some other species roses recommended by growers for the north Pacific coast: *R. moschata nepalensis*, a white-blossomed, well-scented Climber that stays in bloom from spring to midsummer; *R.sericea* var. *omeiensis* forma *pteracantha*, grown not for blossoms but for striking, large red thorns; and *R. soulieana*, whose yellow buds open to single white flowers and which is most sought after for its bluish foliage.

Many Species Roses have been crossed with other roses to produce offspring that are referred to as Species Hybrids. This is because, usually, they strongly resemble the species parent. Examples in the maritime Northwest include the very popular yellow climber 'Mermaid', a Hybrid Bracteata, and the white Hybrid Spinossima, 'Stanwell Perpetual'. Both are grouped with Old Garden Roses.

Old Garden Roses

As people grew to appreciate the comely qualities of native roses, they began to cultivate them. The ancient Romans and Greeks cherished roses, and throughout Europe and parts of Asia to the Far East the love of roses flourished. As different species were cultivated together, many natural hybrids occurred. The ability of roses to sport (mutate) also brought about more varieties. The history of roses is rich in legend and lore; many of the famous old roses are still available today.

The group Old Garden Roses, as designated by the American Rose Society, encompasses a range of heirloom varieties. They are generally a tough lot. Most are quite resistant to disease and, except for Chinas and Teas, quite winter hardy. Criticisms might be that the plants sucker and spread, which makes them hard to keep in-bounds, and that they bloom but once a season.

Rose gardener Jean Rogers is enthusiastic about her collection of over 100 Old Garden Rose varieties near Grants Pass, Oregon. "They are just the most wonderful plants in the world. You can feel the elegance and old-world charm from them. Plus," she adds, "they have that lovely old-fashioned fragrance that roses should have, and they aren't as fussy as the modern roses."

GALLICA   Gallicas (French Roses) are among the earliest cultivated roses, grown in Persia as early as the 12th century B.C. A low-growing, single-flowering shrub, progenitor *Rosa gallica*, grew wild throughout much of Europe.

Once thought to be endowed with magical healing powers, the Gallica varieties are best known for their outstanding fragrance. The scent of R. *gallica officinalis*, known as the Apothecary's Rose, is actually intensified after the petals are dried and crushed. The bush grows to about 4 feet high with deep pink, semi-double blossoms. The plants are hardy and tolerant of poor soils.

The bright range of pinks and purplish reds gained these roses the nickname "Mad Gallicas." Most varieties have few thorns and attractive, healthy foliage on canes that form 3- to 5-foot-tall plants. They require minimal pruning and care, and if grown on their own roots, they will sucker enthusiastically.

"Gallicas are strong growing plants," confirms Ray Duskin, an established rosarian in Coos Bay, Oregon. "Many do well here, even on the coast. 'Complicata' is spectacular here, and 'Charles de Mills', 'Tuscany Superb' ['Superb Tuscan'], 'Rosa Mundi', and *officinalis* [Apothecary's Rose] do extremely well."

'Complicata' is also a big favorite of many other plant professionals, including landscape designer Jane Garrison of Issaquah, Washington, who uses it for its pretty smell and because "the clear pink of the blossoms looks very good against the background of green leaves."

DAMASK   Possibly cultivated since around 800 B.C., Damask roses are still well loved today. They are named for the city of Damascus, from which they were most widely distributed beginning in the 1500s.

For centuries, Damasks have been grown for their unsurpassed fragrance. Rose attar is distilled from the petals of Damask roses, among others, and is the basic ingredient of some of the world's most expensive perfumes. "Nothing compares to them for fragrance," says Jean Rogers.

Damasks bloom in colors from white to wine red in loosely arranged double or semi-double blossoms that occur in long clusters. Bushes from 4 to 6 feet tall grow in an elegant, arching habit, performing best in good soils. Foliage is bright green and fairly disease resistant. Summer Damasks bloom once per summer, and Autumn Damasks produce a flush of fall flowers, in addition to their summer bloom. Bottle-shaped hips add fall interest.

ALBA   Here is a grand old rose. By the 16th century, Albas were a fixture in European rose gardens. This is a rose of outstanding vigor, disease resistance, and stamina. It thrives in poor soil, bad weather, even partial shade. Although it requires little care and minimal pruning, its beauty commands attention and admiration. Lush gray-green foliage sets off a summer wave of blossoms in soft shades of pink. Some varieties of this wonderfully fragrant class rival the Centifolias for fullness of flower. The bushes grow from 4 to 6 feet in height and will spread vigorously if allowed.

Lee Misenheimer is the horticulturalist for Wayside Gardens, a large mail-order rose house in South Carolina. He feels that Albas are among the best possible choices for home gardeners. "Even though they are only in bloom for a few weeks of the year, they are beautiful plants. The foliage is so attractive it makes a wonderful backdrop for other plants to follow."

CENTIFOLIA   The darlings of the Victorian era were the Centifolias, known as cabbage roses because of their huge, petal-packed blossoms. The plants have a graceful, arching shape, with canes bending from the weight of the blooms. The richly fragrant flowers bloom in shades from faint rose to deep pink, into blossoms so full the petals must fold around themselves at the center.

Most Centifolia varieties are well endowed with thorns and form large, lax bushes that benefit from staking. Free-standing dwarf varieties are available and all require little pruning. As a group, Centifolias are fairly resistant to blackspot but susceptible to powdery mildew.

MOSS ROSE   In the early 1700s, nature played a prank on *Rosa centifolia*. A sport (mutation) appeared with a peculiar fuzz covering the buds and base of the flowers. The rose itself was lovely and was dubbed 'Old Pink Moss' (also called 'Communis') for the moss-like bristles that covered the upper stems. Thus began the unusual Moss Roses. They like the mild Northwest climate, but some varieties do not fare well near the sea.

Moss Roses are much like their parent, Centifolias, with the same arching growth habit and similar flowers. The buds and blossoms, however, have the very distinctive coverings of green or brownish glandular projections that give them the mossy appearance. These secrete a sticky, fragrant substance that adds to the scent of the already fragrant flowers.

'Henri Martin' is a Moss Rose often recommended for the north Pacific coast. "An excellent plant, all the way around," says Charles Price. "It is probably the best Moss Rose for the entire area. Even rain doesn't seem to bother it." 'Lemon Delight' and 'Scarlet Moss' are miniature Mosses suitable for patio planters.

Old Garden Rose Favorites

White/White Blend

'Alba Suaveolens' A w
'Blush Noisette' N w
'Boule de Neige' B w
'Leda' D w
'Madame Alfred Carrière' N w
'Madame Hardy' D w

Yellow

'Lady Hillingdon' T yb
'Mutabilis' Ch yb
'Rêve d'Or' N my
'Rosette Delizy' T yb

Pink/Pink Blend

'Apothecary's Rose' G dp
'Catherine Mermet' T lp
'Chloris' A lp
'Communis' ('Old Pink Moss')
    M mp
'Complicata' G pb
'Comte de Chambord' P pb
'Crested Moss' M mp
'Duchesse de Brabant' T lp

'Fantin-Latour' C lp
'Félicité Parmentier' A lp
'Hermosa' Ch lp
'Honorine de Brabant' B pb
'Königin von Dänemark' A mp
'La Reine Victoria' B mp
'La Ville de Bruxelles' D dp
'Madame Isaac Pereire' B dp
'Marquise Boccella' P lp
'Old Blush' Ch mp
'Rosa Mundi' G pb striped
'Petite de Hollande' C mp
'Rose de Rescht' D dp

Red/Red Blend

'Ferdinand Pichard' HP rb
'Henri Martin' M mr
'Hugh Dickson' HP mr

Mauve/Mauve Blend

'Charles de Mills' G m
'Superb Tuscan' G m
'Tour de Malakoff' C m
'William Lobb' M m

CHINA AND TEA   China made two important contributions to Western rose culture with the introduction of China and Tea Roses in the 1800s. These are closely related and share their ability to repeat bloom. The unusual scent of a Tea Rose was compared to that of the tea merchant's goods. The fragrance, along with its distinctly shaped blossoms, soon made Tea Roses a popular choice.

Tea Rose blossoms range in color from white to yellow to shades of pink, tending to nod on their stems. As with China Roses, they are not winter hardy, a trait they have passed on to much of their progeny. 'Lady Hillingdon' is an apricot yellow climbing sport that blooms throughout the summer and fall; it is richly scented and remarkably winter hardy—enough for Cascade winters. 'Catherine Mermet' excels in hot weather, producing large doubles. The compact 'Rosette Delizy' is one of the best Tea Roses. It produces luciously tea-scented, red-rimmed yellow blooms on disease-free plants.

NOISETTE   Among the first China hybrids were the Noisette Roses, named for their famous rose breeder. The result of a cross with *Rosa moschata* (the Musk Rose), 'Blush Noisette' was introduced in the early 1800s. Like other Noisette varieties, this pioneer was noted for its continuously produced, clove-scented clusters of flowers. Several varieties are still available today in white, yellow, pink, and red. They may be grown as open bushes or trained upward. Unfortunately, because of their China parentage, they are not hardy enough for mountain areas.

BOURBON   Another important China hybrid was discovered in 1817 on the Ile de Bourbon (now called Réunion) in the Indian Ocean. It was the result of a natural cross between a resident China and a nearby Autumn Damask, and dubbed Bourbon for its island home.

The Bourbon Roses were all the rage of the Victorian era. The full, globe-shaped flowers are richly scented and most varieties freely produce from summer until winter. The plants are very strong, with arching canes that may reach over 6 feet tall. Although not extremely cold hardy, they fare well from the Cascades west, but most require good soil to do their best.

Many favorite Bourbon varieties from yesteryear are still popular today in the maritime Northwest. The large purplish-pink 'Madame Isaac Pereire' is a special favorite of Charles Price: "It is a very voluptuous and fragrant rose, a bit prone to mildew."

PORTLAND   Timing was the downfall of more than one fine rose, as other, more remarkable varieties appeared to claim the public eye. Such was the fate of the Portland Roses, believed to be the result of a natural cross between an Autumn Damask and *Rosa gallica*. They were an exquisite group with deep-colored, smallish blossoms on compact, bushy plants that bloomed incessantly through the summer. A few of these strong, healthy plants have survived the rose trends to this day. 'Comte de Chambord', a pink blend, is popular in the maritime Northwest.

HYBRID PERPETUAL   One of the first intentional hybrids, the Hybrid Perpetual is considered to be an Old Garden Rose. This masterful accomplishment of plant engineering soon came to overshadow other roses of the 1800s. Hybrid Perpetuals flower prolifically with immense, old-style cabbage rose blooms. More than 4,000 varieties were introduced during the heyday of this rose, which has a somewhat coarse growing habit, is fairly disease resistant, and remains reasonably hardy. A range of reds and pinks is available. Many fine, fragrant varieties perform well in Northwest gardens.

Hybrid Roses

Technically, all but the species roses are hybrids—the result of two separate parents. Most of the Old Garden Roses just mentioned had diverse, often untraceable backgrounds, however. But once their caretakers finally figured out how to manipulate their reproduction, the realm of roses began an expansion that may never subside. The following hybrids appear in order of their appearance in the rose world.

HYBRID TEA   The modern version of the rose incarnate is the Hybrid Tea Rose. Nearly every Old Garden Rose played a part in reaching this pinnacle of rosedom, including the Tea Roses imported from China and the multi-pedigreed Hybrid Perpetuals. Beginning in 1867 with the introduction of 'La France', Hybrid Teas have ridden the crest of stardom like no other rose before them.

Hybrid Teas are usually double-blossomed roses that appear in waves throughout the summer and into autumn. Most often, flowers are borne singly on straight stems, making them the world's favorite cut flowers. The inexhaustible range of colors includes pure icy white, cream, yellow, apricot, orange, pink, red, purple, blends, and bicolors. They require prudent pruning to look their best.

The classic Tea Rose flower form is so popular that old-fashioned roses are often rejected as no longer fitting the image of what many expect a rose to look like. This is tragic, for as lovely as these long-stemmed beauties are, they give roses their reputation for being difficult to grow. Many are not very hardy and are often more susceptible to diseases than other roses, although there are many fine exceptions.

"Despite what people may have you believe," says Jackson & Perkins's Ron Ferguson, "many, many Hybrid Teas excel in the Pacific Northwest. They might make you work for them, but they grow wonderfully."

Hybrid Tea Favorites

White/White Blend
'Honor' w
'Pascali' w
'Pristine' w

Yellow
'Graceland' my
'Irish Gold' my
'Peace' yb

Apricot Blend
'Brandy' ab
'Just Joey' ab

Orange/Orange Blend
'Folklore' ob
'Fragrant Cloud' or
'Las Vegas' ob
'Voodoo' ob

Pink/Pink Blend
'Brigadoon' pb
'Chicago Peace' pb
'Dainty Bess' lp
'Electron' dp
'Silver Jubilee'pb
'Tiffany' pb

Red/Red Blend
'Double Delight' rb
'Granada' rb
'Harry Hastings' dr
'Olympiad' mr
'Papa Meilland' dr
'Perfect Moment' rb
'Precious Platinum' mr

Mauve/Mauve Blend
'Paradise' m

Some of the best Hybrid Teas are European roses that are bred for conditions such as ours. Breeders such as Kordes (Germany), Dickson (Ireland), McGredy (formerly Ireland, now New Zealand), and Meilland (France) produced many of the best-performing roses for the Northwest, from foothills to ocean-side.

One of the most famous imports, the enduring 'Peace' rose from the Meillands of France, is a winner of virtually all major rose awards. Its long-lasting, sweet-scented flowers bloom in a creamy shade of yellow edged in pink on attractive, robust plants.

POLYANTHA AND FLORIBUNDA Small, bushy roses that burst into clusters of bright blossoms were introduced early in the 20th century as Polyanthas, from which developed the distinct Floribunda class. Fragrance was not one of the strong suits, but a surprising clarity of color, magnified by the masses of blooms, certainly was. New rose colors,

Polyantha and Floribunda Favorites

White/White Blend

'Class Act' F w
'French Lace' F w
'Iceberg' F w (not for coast)

Yellow

'Gold Badge' F my
'Red Gold' S yb
'Sun Flare' F my
'Sunsprite' F dy

Apricot Blend

'Amber Queen' F ab
'Apricot Nectar' F ab

Orange/Orange Blend

'Dicky' F op
'First Edition' F op
'Impatient' F or
'Trumpeter' F or

Pink/Pink Blend

'Betty Prior' F mp
'Cecile Brunner' Pol lp
'The Fairy' Pol lp
'Gruss an Aachen' F lp
'Sexy Rexy' F mp

Red/Red Blend

'Europeana' F dr
'Eyepaint' F rb
'Lavaglut' F dr
'Playboy' F rb
'Priscilla Burton' F rb

Mauve/Mauve Blend

'Angel Face' F m
'Purple Tiger' F m

including a golden salmon, a true blood red, and very near blue, popped up quickly to endear these everblooming beauties. Hybridizing was now a sophisticated pursuit, and many exciting new varieties were produced.

A name that means "floriferous in abundance" certainly does Floribundas justice. Some individual flowers closely resemble those of Hybrid Teas. Mass plantings offer constant color.

"I'm really partial to Floribundas," reveals noted rose grower Phil Edmunds of Edmunds' Roses in Wilsonville, Oregon. "With all that bloom they can really dress up a home tremendously." One of his favorites is the variety 'Dicky', a tall, coral orange with clean, disease-resistant foliage. Bob Gold recommends 'Lavaglut', the very fragrant 'Sunsprite', and 'Priscilla Burton'.

Grandiflora Favorites

Yellow
'Gold Medal' Gr my
'Shining Hour' Gr dy

Orange/Orange Blend
'Prominent' Gr or

Pink/Pink Blend
'Pink Parfait' Gr pb

'Queen Elizabeth' Gr mp
'Tournament of Roses' Gr mp

Red/Red Blend
'Love' Gr rb

Mauve/Mauve Blend
'Lagerfeld' Gr m

GRANDIFLORA This somewhat arbitrary category was established to accommodate the lovely rose 'Queen Elizabeth', an uncommonly beautiful Floribunda with large, constantly blooming pink flowers. The Grandifloras that followed were mostly a mix of Floribunda and Hybrid Tea parentage that tends to combine the qualities of both. They are generally large, upright, bushy plants that flower continuously from spring through fall, either singly or in small clusters. Grandifloras are hardy enough for the maritime Northwest climate, though some are more disease resistant than others.

Modern Shrub

A diverse group of landscape roses is loosely grouped as Shrub Roses, which are usually taller or wider than most Hybrid Teas or Floribundas. These include Hybrid Musks, Hybrid Rugosas, Hybrid Moyesiis, English (David Austin) Roses, Kordesiis (from the German breeder), and various other hybrids not addressed here.

Many Shrubs were bred from Hybrid Teas or Floribundas and exhibit the same flower forms and production. There is a range of growth habits from low-growing types to climbers, with many varieties perfectly suited for use as colorful hedges or screens.

HYBRID MUSK The ancient Musk Rose, *Rosa moschata*, lends both its name and heritage to the Hybrid Musks through a long and indirect line. These are strong, disease-resistant roses that produce warmly fragrant flowers in colors from white to apricot yellow to brazen pink. They produce a strong June bloom, in forms from single through fully double, then repeat throughout the summer if encouraged through minimal pruning. Hybrid Musks are generally easy-care roses that, unlike many hybrids, are quite hardy.

Nursery horticulturist Lee Misenheimer lists 'Nymphenburg' and 'Buff Beauty' as strongest growers, and joins others to recommend 'Kathleen', which can be viewed in a frequently photographed arbor at Tacoma's Lakewold. "They are very popular in [the Northwest] region and practically immune to mildew," he says.

HYBRID RUGOSA   It is little wonder that Hybrid Rugosas are favorites among those who wish to grow trouble-free roses. They flourish in the face of the harshest conditions, including salty sea breezes, poor sandy soil or clay, and neglect.

The many varieties bloom throughout the season in a spectrum of colors and flower types, sometimes found in the Old Garden Rose group. The lovely double white 'Blanc Double de Coubert' produces large, fragrant blossoms spring through fall. 'Charles Albanel' is a new variety with semi-double, mauve-red flowers that bloom continuously from spring through fall. Like most Rugosas, it is hardy and practically untouched by disease.

If you have had bad luck in the past with yellow roses, Lee Misenheimer recommends 'Topaz Jewel', an everblooming, very disease-tolerant Rugosa hybrid.

'Thérèse Bugnet' and 'Hansa' are favorites of Raintree Nursery's owner Sam Benowitz. Of 'Alba' he says, "It has beautiful, as well as lasting, white flowers and it grows like crazy in western Washington." Dan Borroff, noted for his specialty of integrating drought-resistant plants, also recommends 'Hansa' and 'Frau Dagmar Hartopp'.

An exceptionally nice, disease-resistant variety developed in Canada to tolerate extreme cold is 'David Thompson', a compact Hybrid Rugosa bush that requires little care but produces fragrant, red flowers all summer long.

Prune occasionally to maintain an attractive plant and encourage bloom. As the flowers fade and fall, the Rugosas' autumn encore of bright orange-red hips takes the stage for a sparkling winter show in your garden.

Shrub Favorites

White/White Blend

'Blanc Double de Coubert'
  HRg w
'Fair Bianca' S (Austin) w

Yellow

'Golden Wings' S ly
'Graham Thomas' S (Austin) dy
'Topaz Jewel' HRg my

Apricot Blend

'Buff Beauty' HMsk ab
'Sweet Juliette' S (Austin) ab

Orange/Orange Blend

'All that Jazz' S ob

Pink/Pink Blend

'Abraham Darby' S (Austin) pb
'Belinda' HMsk mp
'Bonica' S mp
'Cerise Bouquet' S dp
'Constance Spry' S (Austin) lp

'Frau Dagmar Hartopp' HRg mp
'Gertrude Jekyll' S (Austin) mp
'Heritage' S (Austin) lp
'Kathleen' HMsk lp
'Nymphenburg' HMsk pb
'Penelope' HMsk lp
'Pink Meidiland' S pb
'Thérèse Bugnet' HRg mp
'Vanity' HMsk dp

Red/Red Blend

'Charles Albanel' HRg mr
'David Thompson' HRg mr
'F. J. Grootendorst' HRg mr
'Geranium' HMoy mr
'Hansa' HRg mr
'Othello' S (Austin) m
'Ruskin' HRg dr
'Scarlet Meidiland' S mr
'Will Scarlet' HMsk mr

Mauve/Mauve Blend

'Rugosa Magnifica' HRg m

HYBRID MOYESII   For an unusual display, Hybrid moyesii are hard to beat. 'Geranium' is the most popular variety. The single, bright scarlet flowers with a fringed center of contrasting yellow bloom in the summer over a background of light green foliage. However, the spectacular display of elongated vivid red hips is the real attention-getter. This large (6 feet or more) bush is nearly immune to blackspot.

ENGLISH ROSES   David Austin is one of the recognized contemporary rose breeders whose contributions are important to rose lovers on the north Pacific coast. Known both as David Austin Roses and English Roses, these are created from an assortment of parent stock, including many fabulous Old Garden Roses (for vigor, flower, form, and fragrance) and Floribundas (for color and profuse flowering habit). Flower colors range from the pure white 'Fair Bianca' to the rich yellow 'Graham Thomas' and a wealth of pinks and reds. Most are deliciously fragrant.

Austin's English Roses are terminal bloomers, which means there won't be flowers up and down the plant. Although they are very vigorous growers, most really stretch in their second and third years, growing into very large plants. Growth is usually bushy and upright, expanding over time into a large, lax form if left uncut. Though bred for disease resistance, some, such as 'Fair Bianca', must be sprayed for mildew, while others, such as the intensely fragrant 'Abraham Darby', need protection from blackspot.

Rose breeders such as Wilhelm Kordes of Germany and the Meillands of France have devoted decades to creating attractive, low-maintenance roses. Much emphasis has been put on hardiness, disease resistance, vigor, and, of course, beauty. Most types produce multitudes of small, usually fragrant blossoms in forms from single to fully double and from Tea-shaped to full old rose blooms. There are many exceptional varieties, such as the shade-tolerant 'Scarlet Meidiland', the vibrant orange blend 'All That Jazz', the Floribunda-like 'Bonica', and the pink blend shrub 'Carefree Wonder'.

Ramblers and Climbers

Roses that produce long canes may be called Ramblers or Climbers. A Rambler, a class in itself, generally blooms but once a season on canes produced the previous year. Many Climbers bloom repeatedly throughout the season on new wood.

Ramblers are characterized by soft canes, averaging from 15 to 20 feet long, which are covered by tiny flowers in the spring. Since flowers grow on last season's wood, wait to prune until they finish flowering. Sturdy support is needed for these rambunctiously vigorous growers, but this adds interest when part of the garden architecture.

Throughout the maritime Northwest, Rambler varieties such as 'Dorothy Perkins' and 'American Pillar' can be found scrambling up trees, over arbors, and onto the eaves of large porches on some grand old homes.

'Chevy Chase', a newcomer among Ramblers, is considered by many to be one of the best, in part because of the profusion of tiny, red

Rambler and Climber Favorites

White/White Blend

'Sombreuil' ClT w
'Swan Lake' LCl w
'White Dawn' LCl w

Yellow/Yellow Blend

'Mermaid' ClHBc my
'Peace, Cl.' ClHT yb

Apricot Blend

'Alchymist' S ab
'Royal Sunset' LCl ab

Orange-Pink

'America' LCl op
'Dainty Bess, Cl.' ClHT lp
'Dr. W. VanFleet' LCl lp
'Jeanne Lajoie' ClMin mp

Red/Red Blend

'Altissimo' LCl mr
'American Pillar' R pb
'Blaze' LCl mr
'Chevy Chase' R dr
'Étoile de Hollande' ClHT mr
'Handel' LCl rb
'Joseph's Coat' LCl rb

flowers that cover the canes in early summer. Most Ramblers are some-what susceptible to mildew, but this is an exception.

"There are so many outstanding Climbers," says Phil Edmunds, "but if I had to pick a favorite it would probably be the single, red 'Altissimo'." It is also the favorite of Bob Gold and Cynthia Holdren, whose roses consistently place at the top in regional and national competitions. According to Gold, "It produces sprays of saucer-shaped red velvet flowers set off by golden stamens. In one arrangement, they were one of the longest-lasting cut flowers, and lasted up to four weeks, while Hybrid Teas in the same arrangement were changed weekly."

Large-Flowered, or everblooming, Climbers are extraordinarily vigorous plants. Shorter varieties are often referred to as pillar roses, as their comparatively shorter canes are best suited for training up a pillar or post. Many long-caned Climbers produce fewer flowers than other roses, partly because they use so much of their resources to produce growth. Most also tend to produce fewer flowers, usually only at the tips of the canes, if they are forced to grow upright. An arched or horizontal position will coax more flowering buds along the length of the canes.

If you have a favorite variety in bush form, it is likely that you can also find a climbing form. Some are very fragrant, and most are hardy and disease resistant. 'Royal Sunset', a Portland Gold Medal winner for regional excellence, is a nice choice, giving out a fruity scent as it climbs along your garden fence or wall. 'White Dawn', another Large-Flowered Climber, is one of my favorites. 'Swan Lake', a beautiful white with a hint of pink blush, is also recommended. Another favorite Climber is the Miniature 'Jeanne Lajoie', which produces masses of tiny pink flowers all summer long; it was bred by Seattleite Ed Sima.

Miniature

Diminutive little darlings with all the charm of full-sized roses, Miniatures make certain that there really is room for them in any garden. Minis come in every color of the rose rainbow. Most form dense, compact plants no more than 1 or 2 feet in height. Crossing with other roses has created different types, from the larger 'Jean Kenneally' to the trailing 'Red Cascade'.

Miniatures require much the same care as full-sized roses but on a smaller scale. Their smaller, shallower root systems are more vulnerable to environmental extremes, though a good mulch helps to protect them. Minis are usually grown on their own roots and usually sold growing in containers. They can be grown indoors (where they are susceptible to spider mites) or moved in and out, depending upon the season, if kept in pots.

Some Miniature varieties are so disease free that they require little care other than watering, plus less pruning than full-sized roses. Like big roses, they benefit from full-strength sprays, but care should be taken not to overfertilize them, according to Bob Gold. In raised beds or large planters (such as whiskey barrels), he finds that they grow well and are particularly easy to care for.

My grandmother, Marie Massingham, has been tending her roses for well over six decades now. Much to the delight of her neighbors, she continues to keep extensive borders. Several years ago, the theme of her birthday surprise party was, of course, roses. Everyone brought a gift of a different Miniature. Though she had tried them before, this was the first chance she had to experiment with many different varieties. Since then, Miniatures have become her favorite, and for reasons that may not surprise you. "They are so cute, those little guys," she says, "but what I really like is that they are a lot less trouble to work around. They don't reach out and grab you like the bigger roses do!"

Miniature Favorites

White/White Blend

'Gourmet Popcorn' Min w
'Snowfall' ClMin w

Yellow/Yellow Blend

'Lemon Delight' Min my
'Rise 'n' Shine' Min my

Apricot Blend

'Jean Kenneally' Min ab
'Loving Touch' Min ab

Orange/Orange Blend

'Anytime' Min ob
'Little Jackie' Min ob

Orange Red

'Starina' Min or

Pink/Pink Blend

'Cupcake' Min mp
'Heartbreaker' Min pb
'Jeanne Lajoie' ClMin mp
'Minnie Pearl' Min pb

Red/Red Blend

'Dreamglo' Min rb
'Magic Carrousel' Min rb
'Red Cascade' ClMin dr
'Scarlet Moss' Min mr

Mauve/Mauve Blend

'Winsome' Min m

Dianne Ostergaard, president of the Salem Rose Society in Oregon, adds that in the Willamette Valley her Minis bloom almost all year round. The "favorites" list above includes Dianne's favorites and those of Bob Gold.

STANDARDS (TREE ROSES)   Not constituting a classification unto themselves, standards—commonly called Tree Roses—are the result of the union of two or three separate plants. A tough, thick-growing trunk is grafted onto a flowering variety, which might be grafted onto a third for rootstock. The trunk does not continue to grow, so the rose tree stays the same height. Tree Roses are available in a vast array of flowering forms, including Miniatures, Hybrid Teas, and Climbers that give a weeping tree effect.

Protect them from intense sun or extreme cold by painting trunks with a whitewash or wrapping them. Try wrapping with R-11 attic insulation diagonally all the way to the root, then making a loose, bowl-like collar around the leaves, leaving the top open for air.

"My only regret about Tree Roses," says nurseryman Ned Wells, "is the varieties that are commonly available. For some reason, everybody wants to graft Hybrid Teas, when Floribundas would fill in so much more nicely."

Just as the types of roses are diverse, so are the qualities they have to offer. The next chapter delves into these qualities to help you choose just the right rose—or roses—for your garden.

Selections for Your Garden

CHAPTER 2

What do you picture as the perfect rose for your garden? A grand, sprawling Climber cascading over an arbor? A neat row of tidy bushes topped with bright 5-inch blossoms along the driveway? Perhaps you favor the everblooming qualities of a Floribunda to mark the edge of the lawn. Maybe you only have room for a sparkling Miniature.

Reduce the demands your roses place on your time by planting Hybrid Rugosas or landscape Shrub Roses. Also rely on low-maintenance varieties such as 'The Fairy' (a Polyantha), many Albas, Rugosas, or other landscape roses. Whatever your individual needs, the inherent diversity of the rose world ensures that at least one rose will suit your purposes.

When people discuss what qualities they desire in a rose, color and flower form are often the first mentioned. The ultimate size of the plant is an important consideration for limited spaces. A fragrant rose is a double delight, and some roses are also remarkable for their fragrant foliage.

Roses with bright hips, red stems, and fall color can extend the landscape value of roses well into the winter. Natural disease resistance should also be on your list of priorities. Choose your roses for what pleases you, but be aware that some demand more attention, effort, and expense to maintain than others that serve the same purpose.

DECIDING ON COLOR

What strikes us first about a rose is the color of the flowers. We see them from a distance and are drawn closer. The blossom shade is often the first thing we consider when picking out a new variety. It has to suit our tastes and our existing landscape. Thanks to the wide selection of roses available, you are sure to find a few shades to complement your home landscape.

Roses come in shades of white, yellow, orange, pink, mauve, and red, with many blends and bicolors. Dozens of them are fine roses for a maritime Northwest garden. Roses on the lists of favorites throughout this book are color coded.

Ron Ferguson of Jackson & Perkins confirms that red is one of the most popular colors for roses (although he reports that unusual colors, such as the purple-and-white Floribunda 'Purple Tiger', are beginning to challenge reds in popularity). Among his personal favorites are the Hybrid Teas 'Legend' and 'Olympiad'; 'Olympiad' is widely acclaimed as an "all-weather" rose. Coos Bay, Oregon, rosarian Jay Dow also recommends the Hybrid Tea 'Alec's Red' for the extreme coast.

Many factors can affect the depth and quality of color. Growing conditions can influence hue. The same variety grown in two different locales may display markedly different shades. Flower color may also change during the course of the blooming season. Many reds, such as 'Mr. Lincoln', are notorious for fading or "bluing" as they age. 'Precious Platinum' is a good unfading red. For most roses, new blooms are usually a deeper shade than older flowers.

Buds may be an entirely different color than the opened flower, especially among bicolor roses. This creates a multicolored tapestry of blooms as the plant fills with blossoms at different stages of opening. 'Handel' (cream with hot pink edges) and 'Joseph's Coat', frequently recommended Large-Flowered Climbers for the maritime Northwest, are examples. The canes of 'Joseph's Coat' ignite into red and yellow flickers of color as the petals of each blossom unfold.

CHOOSING FLOWER FORM

The form of the bloom, as well as the overall growth habit of the plant, sets the tone of the garden. The blossom form accentuates the color as light and shadow play across the petals. The curves and valleys of the surface reflect not only the hue, but also something more visceral. Huge, nodding old-fashioned roses evoke nostalgia. Elegant Hybrid Teas lend a more formal feeling. The understated single blooms of Species roses or Hybrid Teas, such as 'Dainty Bess', may be worked into either an old-fashioned or a formal scheme, or woven into the fiber of a wild-like, native planting.

WORKING WITH GROWTH HABIT

Ultimate size should figure prominently in your calculations. Old roses and Ramblers, especially when grown on their own suckering roots, can take over as much ground as their roots can push through. Also, roses labeled as "vigorous growers" grow fast—just how fast depends on the variety and the growing conditions. If you have a large area to cover or unlimited space to let your roses roam, then this may be the quality you seek. When logistics dictate a smaller scale, look for varieties labeled "compact."

Be realistic about how much space you can devote to your roses, because they are not going to change their growing habits easily. For healthy growth, allow enough space between them and any other plants or structures for good air circulation. The amount of space depends on the varieties grown.

The smaller varieties are ideal for edging beds or foundation plantings, and the grand scale of the larger growing varieties makes them more suitable for filling in corners or heralding large entryways. Some shrub-type roses lend themselves well to planting close to form hedges. Larger Hybrid Rugosa hedges are effective as property boundaries, yet softer in appearance than a solid fence.

INDULGE IN FRAGRANCE

Trick question: If you get into a scrape and come out smelling like a rose, how, exactly, do you smell? Next to color, the fragrance of roses has held an undeniable allure for us since ancient times, but oh, to describe the scent.

Rose scents promenade up and down the scale of intensity. Many modern roses have lost their scent, leaving nothing to endear them but a pretty face. Almost any type of rose has fragrant varieties, but the Old Garden Roses, such as Damasks, Centifolias, and Albas, are among the most aromatic.

When you stop and smell the roses, the perfume that greets you may not be what you expected. Rugosas smell of cinnamon or cloves. Musk Roses smell of warm honey (not of musk oxen). Some, such as the English (= Austin) Rose 'Abraham Darby', have a fruity aroma. 'Cerise Bouquet' is a Shrub Rose with a raspberry fragrance. Tea Roses were named for their tea-like scent. There are roses with a citrus aroma, a warm spicy scent like myrrh, and the smell of licorice. And don't overlook the pine-scented, bristly buds of the Moss Roses or the apple-scented foliage of the Sweetbriar Roses.

"Some of my personal favorites for fragrance are not necessarily the most naturally disease resistant," laments Scott Stiles of Raintree Nursery. "I like 'Abraham Darby', 'Mr. Lincoln', and 'Fragrant Cloud', but all of them can be horribly prone to blackspot. There are many Rugosa cultivars that are fragrant and are more naturally disease resistant." Heronswood Nursery's Dan Hinkley especially likes the Hybrid Rugosa 'Blanc Double de Coubert'.

"Hybrid Musks," advises Lee Misenheimer, "are often fragrant and are usually very strong growers. 'Kathleen' is not only fragrant, but also it doesn't get mildew." Cut back Hybrid Musks in late winter to encourage further fragrant bloom.

Old roses, especially Damasks and Gallicas, in part owe their longevity to their head-turning fragrances. Damasks 'La Ville de Bruxelles' and 'Rose de Rescht' and Gallica 'Charles de Mills' are names that turn up frequently in discussions of fragrant old roses for the Northwest. Many Albas, such as 'Königin von Dänemark', 'Félicité Parmentier', and 'Alba Suaveolens', are also regional favorites for their old-time aromas. Moss Roses 'Communis' and 'Crested Moss' produce lushly scented blooms valued by area gardeners.

Ramblers, Climbers, and Species Roses are often very fragrant. The gardenia-like blooms of 'White Dawn' (a Large-Flowered Climber) are among my favorites. 'Sombreuil', a Climbing Tea, has been used successfully by the landscape design firm of Withey-Price in the Seattle area. The ever-present 'Dr. W. Van Fleet', parent of 'White Dawn', is a nicely scented Rambler that has called the north Pacific coast home longer than many pioneer families.

Hybrid Teas have some strongly scented varieties, despite the common complaint that modern roses have had the scent bred out of them. Salem Rose Society president Dianne Ostergaard recommends the deep, wine-like aroma of 'Sweet Surrender'.

Veteran rose gardener Albert Keel of Butchart Gardens in Victoria, B.C., favors 'Papa Meilland'. Along with 'Double Delight', 'Sheer Bliss' is high on Ron Ferguson's list of favorite fragrant roses grown by Jackson & Perkins. Rich Baer, editor of the *Portland Rose Society Newsletter*, foresees the new variety 'New Zealand' as a great choice of fragrant rose for the maritime Northwest. And when Mike and Rhea

Top: 'F. J. Grootendorst', a Hybrid Rugosa with carnation-like blooms. **Bottom left**: *Rosa moyesii* hips complement blue-gray *Artemisia* 'Powis Castle'; both plants are water-wise for the maritime Northwest. **Bottom right**: Sweetbriar roses, which have apple-scented leaves.

Top left: A Hybrid Musk fronted by an *Allium giganteum* globe and white *Corydalis*. **Top right**: Clusters of semi-double flowers fill 'Bonica', a good hedge rose that blooms all season. **Bottom**: Moss Mini 'Dresden Doll' features mossy-looking, fragrant projections.

Top: The showy Climbing Hybrid Tea 'Tropicana' started as an inexpensive boxed rose from a chain nursery. **Bottom**: The Hybrid Tea 'Etoile de Hollande' is fragrant as well as beautiful. **Following page**: Ascending the fence is a Large-Flowered Climber, 'Royal Sunset'.

Top: Outstanding among the Hybrid Teas is the popular 'Dainty Bess', also available as a 10-foot-tall Climber. **Bottom**: One of the most enduring Portland Gold Medal winners, the Hybrid Tea 'Peace', with a pink hybrid lily.

Top left: 'Fragrant Cloud', a Portland Gold Medal–winning Hybrid Tea recommended for the maritime Northwest. **Top right**: 'Brandy', another Hybrid Tea, is a favorite All-American Rose Selection. **Bottom left**: Versatile yellow Shrub Rose 'Golden Wings'. **Bottom right**: 'Fanfare', a Floribunda double with 20 to 30 petals.

Top: In front of the birdbath are 'Sweet Surrender', a pink Miniature, and 'Sun Sprite', a favorite yellow Floribunda touted by Northwest gardeners. **Bottom left**: 'Playboy', a Floribunda awarded the Portland Gold Medal for regional excellence. **Bottom right**: Award-winning 'Toy Clown', a Miniature.

Top: Pink Floribunda Mini 'Bella Rosa', a Kordesii from Germany, and 'Gertrude Jekyll', a fragrant, pink Austin (English) Rose, combine old-fashioned charm with disease resistance. **Bottom left**: *Rosa pteracantha* thorns punctuate perennial borders. **Bottom right**: 'Tournament of Roses', an excellent Grandiflora.

Fragrant Favorites

Pleasing scents can be found throughout all rose classifications in all colors. The James Alexander Gamble Rose Fragrance Medal is awarded to otherwise outstanding roses that are also "strongly and delightfully fragrant." Gamble Medal Winners that thrive in the coastal Northwest have an asterisk (*).

White/White Blend

'Alba Suaveolens' A w
'Blanc Double de Coubert' HRg w
'Blush Noisette' N w
'Boule de Neige' B w
'Cinderella' Min w
'Garden Party' HT w
'Madame Hardy' D w
'Sheer Bliss' HT w
'White Dawn' LCl w
'White Lightnin'' Gr w

Yellow/Yellow Blend

*'Sunsprite' F dy

Apricot Blend

'Amber Queen' F ab
'Brandy' HT ab
'Buff Beauty' HMsk ab
'Just Joey' HT ab

Orange/Orange Blend

'Starina' Min or

Orange Red

*'Fragrant Cloud' HT or

Pink/Pink Blend

'Abraham Darby' S pb
'Aotearoa New Zealand' HT lp
'City of London' F lp
'Cerise Bouquet' S dp
'Communis' M mp
'Complicata' G pb
'Comte de Chambord' P pb
'Crested Moss' M mp
'Duchesse de Brabant' T lp
Rosa eglanteria Sp lp
'Félicité Parmentier' A lp
'Gertrude Jekyll' S mp
'Gruss an Aachen' F lp
'Honorine de Brabant' B pb
'Kathleen' HMsk lp
'Königin von Dänemark' A mp
'La Ville de Bruxelles' D dp
'Madame Isaac Pereire' B dp
'Nymphenburg' HMsk pb
'Penelope' HMsk lp
'Petite de Hollande' C mp
'Queen Elizabeth' Gr mp
'Rose de Rescht' D dp
'Sweet Surrender' HT mp
*'Tiffany' HT pb
'Vanity' HMsk dp

Red/Red Blend

'Beauty Secret' Min mr
*'Double Delight' HT rb
*'Granada' HT rb
*'Papa Meilland' HT dr

Mauve/Mauve Blend

'Angel Face' F m
'Intrigue' F m
'Lagerfeld' Gr m
Rosa rugosa S m and hybrids
'Sachet' Min m
'Tuscany Superb' G m
'Tour de Malakoff' C m
'William Lobb' M m

Pearsall of Lebanon, Oregon, wanted to start the perfect rose garden in their new home, they relied on the wonderful scent and solid reputation of 'Granada' as their first choice.

It is no surprise, then, that we have long sought to capture elusive essence of roses, often preserving them in potpourris or perfumes. Attar of roses has long been a staple of the perfume industry. Damasks or Albas are commonly used for attar; the French prefer *Rosa centifolia*. It takes an average of an acre of roses to produce a pound of precious attar.

Fragrance in roses is again in vogue. With it comes a renewed appreciation for many of the richly scented heirloom varieties, and also a rekindled interest in developing new fragrant cultivars. Ron Ferguson notes that people who truly desire that intensely rewarding scent will put up with just about anything—including fussy plants—to get it.

HIPS, CANES, THORNS, AND FOLIAGE

Beautiful blossoms, exquisite fragrance—what more could a rose possibly have to offer? Just look at the rest of the rose.

Whether for fall and winter landscape interest, or for the benefit of overwintering birds and wildlife, consider fruiting roses. Rose fruit (hips) forms when the petals fall and the base of the flower begins to swell. In Species Roses, Rugosas, and other varieties that set fruit, seeds will develop inside these hips. As they ripen, they turn from green to bright orange or red and become thick and fleshy. Hips are high in vitamin C and the bright color attracts winter creatures to the sustaining fruit. Old Garden Roses, Rugosas, and the *moyesii* variety 'Geranium' provide a wealth of eye-catching, life-giving hips.

Old rose bushes may age into a mass of tangled canes and thorns, but even a rose best described as an impenetrable mess has its saving grace. Wild birds will congregate to such a safe haven. Catering to birds need not be altogether altruistic, because many will keep insect pests out of the garden and away from the roses.

The rugosa 'Frau Dagmar Hartopp' produces a brilliant autumn show, complete with bright hips and colorful foliage. The leaves first turn maroon, then a searing metallic yellow. Shrub Rose 'Cerise Bouquet' is noted for its colorful foliage and stems, and the popular Species Roses *Rosa glauca*, *R. soulieana*, and *R. nitida* are also highly valued for their unique and attractive foliage. The full, blue-gray-green leaves of Alba Roses form the perfect backdrop to blooming perennials.

Thorns, or the lack of them, are another point of interest with certain roses. The species *R. sericea* var. *omeiensis* forma *pteracantha* produces scanty flowers but columns of very striking, clear red thorns. "This rose does wonderfully here," assures Dan Hinkley, "and it adds a very unusual point of interest." In contrast, other rose lovers appreciate the nearly naked stems of so-called thornless varieties such as the Bourbon 'Zéphirine Drouhin' and the Alba 'Chloris'.

NATURAL DISEASE RESISTANCE

From Canada to California, some stretches of Interstate 5 may best be described as one long rose bed. This is hardly a pampered position for plants, but most of these roses look pretty good. According to Dr. Russ Rosenthal at the Washington Department of Transportation Beautification, highway roses have to meet a nearly impossible set of standards. He prefers Species Roses to modern roses for the long stretches of roadway he has to cover. "These wild roses are tough. They are not sprayed, watered, or cut back. They have to contend with whatever rose pests and diseases are out there, and yet every year, they come back."

The highway roses are a varied lot, including Rugosa hybrids and Species Roses such as *Rosa nutkana*, *R. woodsii*, and *R. gymnocarpa*, among the most common.

Disease resistance is not insurance that a rose will never be attacked by a fungus, bacteria, or virus—it is just less likely. If afflicted, however, resistant plants will generally suffer much less damage than susceptible varieties. This is vital, because diseases such as blackspot spread rapidly and can defoliate roses with alarming speed. Choose disease-resistant varieties to protect your investment and cut your work load at the same time.

Many varieties require no chemical protection. However, by introducing just one susceptible variety to your rose garden, you invite disease into the presence of all. All the roses listed in this book are disease resistant unless otherwise noted. Ask at your nursery or write to your mail-order nursery's horticulturalist to recommend other disease-resistant varieties for the maritime Northwest and your particular microenvironment.

Selected Portland Gold Medal Winners

White/White Blend

'Class Act' F w
'French Lace' F w
'Honor' HT w
'Pristine' HT w

Yellow

'Irish Gold' HT my
'Sun Flare' F my

Apricot Blend

'Maid of Honor' HT ab

Orange/Orange Blend

'Las Vegas' HT ob
'Tony Jacklin' F o

'Touch of Class' HT op
'Trumpeter' F or

Pink/Pink Blend

'Keepsake' HT pb
'Prima Donna' Gr dp
'Queen Elizabeth' Gr mp
'Sexy Rexy' F mp
'Silver Jubilee' HT pb
'Tiffany' HT pb

Red/Red Blend

'Europeana' F dr
'Love' Gr rb
'Olympiad' HT mr
'Playboy' F rb

HELP FROM RATINGS AND AWARDS

Learn from those who have grown roses before you. Members of the American Rose Society (ARS) from around the United States rate the roses they grow, evaluating the merit of each variety for beauty, health, and vigor. Scores are averaged out to between 1 and 10. Although a lower score indicates that a rose does not perform well in all geographic regions, that rose may excel in the maritime Northwest. A rose that rates high on a national level, however, has proved itself to be dependable in a range of conditions and can be counted on to put on a great show just about anywhere, including here.

The results of the National Rose Ratings are published in an annual pamphlet available from the ARS, *Handbook for Selecting Roses.*

Another indication of a superior rose is the designation AARS (All-American Rose Selection). Chosen from the new varieties introduced each year, AARS are winners evaluated in test gardens across the country. They must meet high standards of prolonged or repeat bloom, disease resistance, and general attractiveness. They must be truly exceptional; in 1951, none qualified. Northwesterners can see AARS winners at the International Rose Test Garden at Washington Park, Portland, and the Woodland Park Rose Garden, Seattle.

Although many AARS winners do well throughout the inland north Pacific coast, many tend to falter along the rarefied environment of the seaside. "Here," confides coastal rose expert Ray Duskin, "we are better off with roses that have won awards in England or places with climates more similar to ours. Royal National Rose Society of England (RNRS) winners do well here. Or look for Portland Gold Medal winners." Some RNRS winners that do well in the maritime Northwest are 'Electron' (a deep pink) and 'Dicky' (an orange pink).

Portland Gold Medal winners are judged along the same lines as AARS winners, but only at the Portland's International Rose Test Garden. They are the cream of the crop for the maritime Northwest. For outstanding fragrance, look for the James Alexander Gamble Rose Fragrance Medal winners on the "Fragrant Favorites" list earlier in this chapter.

CHAPTER 3

A Place for Roses

There is an old saying among real estate agents that there are three things to consider regarding any given piece of property: location, location, and location. This is especially true with the site you choose for your roses. Generally, you can plant two identical rose bushes in two different settings, give them the same care, and almost always see differences in the way they grow and thrive. In fact, the choice of site is often the first explanation as to why a rose does better in someone else's garden than in yours—and from now on, why roses will do better in yours.

FINDING THE BEST SITE

Whether you are dealing with a small city lot or the back forty of a sprawling spread, specific conditions must be considered for your roses. Any size yard or garden has numerous settings that provide distinct micro-environments. Look for a spot that receives plenty of sunshine, is sheltered from prevailing winds, has good air circulation and water drainage, and allows for the individual space needed by the varieties you wish to plant. Most important, plant your roses where they will please you. They are, after all, here for your well-being—not just the other way around.

SUNSHINE Most roses need at least 6 hours of sunshine per day during the flowering season to bloom to their full, glorious potential. Sunlight can, however, be somewhat of an uncertain commodity in the maritime Northwest. Therefore, make the most of it by positioning roses wisely.

A rose's place in the sun is a place in the sun, from first light to twilight, if possible. Overexposure to sunlight is rarely a problem in this region. In areas with high temperatures and intense sunshine, shelter roses from the afternoon sun by planting them on the southeast side of a sunscreen. A southern exposure will flood your roses with life-giving light and they will thank you for it with baskets of bloom. Few varieties will tolerate shade. Do not plant roses along the north face of a wall, fence, or trellis. A northwest corner, however, may catch enough early sun for a rose to do well.

Morning sun is healthiest for roses because it helps to dry dew from the foliage, which helps to discourage fungal diseases. If sunlight is scarce in your planting area, try a white painted surface as a backdrop for your plants. Reflected light can help turn a less-than-sunny site into a bright spot for roses.

SHELTER FROM WIND Though less dramatic than storm damage, any prevailing wind takes its toll on roses. Winds speed evaporation from the surface areas of the plants, causing them to compensate by developing a tough, thick cuticle on stems and leaves. However, roses are thirsty plants and may suffer severe dehydration if exposed to constant breezes. A windbreak may be just the break windblown roses need.

The best windbreak allows for a good deal of air movement. A solid object, such as a wall, is fine when the wind is coming from the direction opposite the windbreak. But winds striking the wall from the same side as the roses are forced backwards, creating significant turbulence. A hedge, line of trees, or partially covered trellis will slow advancing winds while allowing them to pass through without backlash. Allow at least 10 feet between roses and a solid windbreak, 4 to 10 feet for a hedge or trellis.

Coastal areas are notorious for brutal winds. In areas where megahold hair spray sells well, consider the effects of air turbulence before planting your roses. The damage inflicted by high storm winds is obvious by broken canes, scattered petals, and shredded foliage. Plants often spring back from storms with amazing vigor, but a little forethought can spare them unnecessary abuse.

In Long Beach, Washington, the Kite Capital of the World, stalwart roses wave defiantly in the near-constant breeze. Those planted along the eastern face of buildings or other structures show little fatigue compared with those dancing in the wind. Protected bushes tend to have fuller foliage and more, longer-lasting blooms.

GOOD AIR CIRCULATION In contrast to strong wind, good air circulation is very beneficial to roses. Air movement through the bush keeps canes and foliage dry, which cuts down on disease. It also offers frost protection. Remember that cold air sinks and collects in low spots, so avoid planting in dips or closed-in spaces that trap air. This is another reason to plant roses on a gentle slope to the south or southeast: the slope is ideal, allowing for air flow, maximum sunlight, and water drainage.

DRAINAGE   Soil that allows for good water drainage is an absolute requirement for roses. Most roses cannot tolerate soggy roots. Luckily, unlike the sun and wind, this is one variable you can somewhat control.

If you are blessed with well-drained soil on a gentle slope, consider yourself lucky. Otherwise, you can improve soil drainage. Amend light, sandy soils that won't hold water with organic matter, or humus. A steep, water-shedding site can be terraced into an outstanding rose display, which provides all the pleasure of a rose garden while serving to eliminate erosion. Heavy soils that drain too slowly also can be vastly improved by adding humus. Solid clay or hardpan subsoil may require that drainage tiles or underground pipes be installed to funnel water away from plant roots. If water stands in pools on your property for days after a rain, the best idea is to relocate your roses.

To determine how well your soil drains, conduct a simple test. Dig a hole about 1 foot wide by 2 feet deep. Fill it to the brim with water and time the drainage rate. If it takes more than 2 hours to drain—and if your soil needs improvement to become friable—reconsider the site or make some changes in soil quality suggested in the next chapter.

INDIVIDUAL SPACING   Each type of rose has different space requirements, due to individual growth habits. Spreading old-fashioned roses obviously require more ground than petite Miniature varieties. Some types climb, claiming little ground space, while others sprawl so well they are used as ground covers. They all look pretty sparse in the bare-root stage at planting time, so know your rose's growing habit before you buy, because it is the ultimate size of the specimen that counts. Hacking an incorrectly spaced rose to conform to unnatural limits is no substitute for giving it the space it deserves.

Growth habit is not the only reason roses need their space. It takes a lot of sunshine, moisture, and nutrition to produce all that royal beauty, and the noble rose does not like to compete for any of it. Shallow-rooted neighbors are generally well tolerated, provided enough water is available for all. Roses won't thrive in the near company of serious competition such as trees, large bushes, or other heavy feeders.

Rose Sizes (in feet)

Rose	Height	Width
Alba	4–6	4–6
Bourbon	4–8	3–6
Centifolia	3–5	4
China	2½–8	3–7
Climber	6–25	varies
Damask	3–6	2½–4
Floribunda	2–4	1½–2½
Gallica	3–5	3–5
Grandiflora	5–6	2½–3
Hybrid Musk	4–15	4–8
Hybrid Perpetual	5	5; more if pegged
Hybrid Tea	3–6	2½–4
Miniature	¾–3	1–3
Mini Standards	1½	1½–2
Noisette	6–12	3–5
Polyantha	2	up to 6
Rambler	to 20+	to 20
Rugosa	5–7	4–8
Shrub Rose	3–7	3–7
Standard (Tree Rose)	3–6	2–3
Tea	2½–7	3–4

FOR JOY! A ROSE. Never lose sight of the only good reason for planting roses in the first place: your own personal satisfaction and enjoyment. Although every landscape is different, there are usually one or two areas in your yard that get the most traffic. Think of these outside "rooms" as you do your favorite rooms inside your home. Don't they deserve a little sprucing up?

Some favorite spots for roses include walkways, entryways, a corner off the back door, along a deck or patio, and near a backyard gazebo. The view from the kitchen window can be transformed from mundane to exquisite by planting roses so that the window frames their setting. Take advantage of the lovely colors and uplifting fragrances to lift your spirits at every opportunity. Read more about incorporating roses into your yard in Chapter 10, on rosescaping. Meanwhile, plant your roses where you will see—and smell—them!

To get the most out of your roses:

Look for:	*Avoid:*
Full sun	Shade
Gentle slope	Bottom of a hill
Southern exposure	Northern exposure
Shelter from prevailing wind	Closed-in area
Good drainage	Standing water/quicksand
Adequate space	Crowding/planting near competition

SUCCEEDING IN YOUR MICRO-ENVIRONMENT

Growing environments differ dramatically along the north Pacific coast. A windswept ocean ridge community like Coos Bay, Oregon, stays moderately cool and damp all year long, while in inland Roseburg the summer heat can be oppressive.

To a lesser degree, differing micro-environments can be found on a much smaller scale—in your yard. Consider all of the factors necessary for the health and well-being of your roses before committing them to any given spot. Even though your yard may lack a perfect site, chances are pretty good that there are some that are better than others.

SEASIDE Ocean-side rosarians point out that many varieties do not fare well in cool, damp, ocean-side climates. They warn against choosing very double varieties (roses with 35 to 40 or more petals) because the flowers often fail to open. Rosarian Jay Dow, of Coos Bay, Oregon, warns that roses from the "Masterpiece Series" are ill-suited for that particular climate. In general, most roses were originally developed in areas with warm, dry summers and so are doomed along the water's edge. Instead, rose lovers from Vancouver Island south to San Francisco Bay suggest ordering roses hybridized in areas of similar growing conditions, such as England or Germany, or ordering from knowledgeable local growers.

Of the roses that flourish at the seaside the type most unanimously acclaimed are the Rugosa hybrids. These strong plants take on all the challenges of the area, including wet weather, wind, and light soil. Other varieties that do well near the surf are listed in the box on the facing page.

CASCADE SLOPE Though temperatures rarely plunge low enough there to be damaging to most roses, frost protection may be necessary for less-than-hardy varieties or during an unusually harsh winter.

Roses for the Seaside

Shrubs and Old Garden Roses

Consulting rosarian Ray Duskin has quite a few favorite Old Garden Roses and Shrub Roses with old-fashioned characteristics that do well in the special conditions of the maritime Northwest coast.

'Abraham Darby' S pb   'Great Maiden's Blush' A w
'Angelica' S dp   'Rosa Mundi' G pb
'Apothecary's Rose' G dp   'Old Red Moss' M mr
'Charles de Mills' G m   'Sweet Juliet' S ab
'Crested Moss' M mp   'Tuscany Superb' G m
'Fair Bianca' S w   'Winchester Cathedral' S w

Modern Varieties

Consulting rosarian Jay Dow recommends favorite Grandifloras, Hybrid Teas, and Floribundas for special coastline conditions.

'Alec's Red' HT mr   'Pascali' HT w
'Brigadoon' HT pb   'Polarstern' HT w
'Elina' HT ly   'Prima Donna' Gr dp
'Elizabeth Taylor' HT dp   'Pristine' HT w
'Irish Gold' HT my   'Queen Elizabeth' Gr mp
'Konrad Henkel' HT mr   'Sun Flare' F my
'Lavaglut' F dr   'Sunsprite' F dy
'Loving Memory' HT mr   'Wimi' HT pb

Again, the best protection is to choose only varieties that are noted for winter hardiness. Purchase roses recommended for U.S. Agricultural Zone 7 or lower. Most roses, except Chinas and Teas, easily meet this requirement.

A problem exists with early-blooming varieties in colder, high-elevation areas such as Langley, B.C., or Sisters, Oregon. Don't plant them where they receive full morning sun, which, in this case, stimulates the bush to break dormancy and begin blooming. Early buds are

Roses for Special Spots

Shade-Tolerant Roses

Albas A
Rosa carolina Sp mp
'Gruss an Aachen' F lp
'Pax' HMsk w
'Scarlet Meidiland' S mr

Wet-Tolerant Roses

Rosa carolina Sp mp
R. gymnocarpa Sp lp
R. nitida Sp mp

Drought-Tolerant Roses

'Fimbriata' HRg lp
Rosa foetida 'Austrian Copper' Sp
'Frau Dagmar Hartopp' HRg mp
'Frühlingsgold' HSpn my
R. glauca Sp mp
'Hansa' HRg mr
R. rugosa species and hybrids
Once-flowering varieties

often killed by hard spring frosts, which leave the stem weakened and likely to die back.

IN BETWEEN   Between the sea and the mountains, the choice of varieties is much broader. Look for the best site possible under the criteria discussed, but don't despair if your site seems totally unworkable. Tough, lovely Rugosa roses can bring the joy of roses to almost any spot. If some shade is unavoidable, try growing Alba Roses, the Floribunda 'Gruss an Aachen', or the shade-tolerant 'Scarlet Meidiland'.

Though most roses die in wet ground, all but the swampiest areas can support the species *Rosa gymnocarpa* and *R. carolina*. Where ground space is limited consider Miniatures or trellised climbing roses. If you can't find a great site for roses, then look for a great rose for your site.

Needs vary from foothills to seaside to ocean ridge. Call local nurseries, write to your local newspaper's garden columnist, or contact your local extension agent for suggestions. Try to preview the varieties you are considering in someone else's yard, a nursery, or a local public garden before planting in yours.

First Prepare the Soil

CHAPTER 4

Once you have decided upon the rose site, it is time to investigate the soil. Scoop up a handful of earth and see what you have to work with. Does it sift through your fingers? If so, the texture is too light and will need improving. Does it stick like goo or is it just plain impossible to scrape up with your hands? Heavy clay or compacted soils are common problems that, happily, are fixable.

Perhaps you are lucky enough to bring up handfuls of dark, sweet-smelling earth that clings lightly, then crumbles as you work it through your fingers. If so, this is the ideal texture for garden soil. Soil like this is the exception and most gardeners must work for it.

EXAMINING THE SOIL

Soil Texture

Differences in soil texture are determined by the size and composition of soil particles, the spaces between them, and the amount of organic matter. Sandy soils consist of larger silica particles, with lots of spaces between and little organic matter. They provide a poor growing medium because they cannot hold water or structurally support plant roots.

Heavy clay soils are made of tightly packed tiny particles with little space in between and, again, insufficient organic matter. Clay holds water all too well, often preventing adequate drainage, which also makes it a poor growing medium, especially for roses.

Test the texture of your soil by filling a jar one-third full of dirt and two-thirds full of water. Shake it vigorously and set it aside. Sand is the heaviest and will settle out first, followed by silt, followed by a layer of clay. Organic matter will float on top. Ideally, about 45 percent should be sand, 35 percent silt, and 20 to 30 percent clay, with the more floating organic matter, the better.

Soil types along the north Pacific coast vary widely. Those along Puget Sound tend to be lighter due to "recent" glacial activity. Much of the Cascade Range and foothills boasts rich volcanic soil, while gardeners from Seattle to Salem often strike sticky red clay. Luckily, almost any type of soil can be vastly improved by adding organic matter, such as compost, rotted manure, or leaf mold. Organic material strengthens sandy soils and creates water retention, while at the same time breaking up clay soils to improve drainage. Gypsum (available at feed stores) also helps to open up heavy clay soils.

pH Levels

Soils in the maritime Northwest have fairly consistent soil acidity (pH). Roses prefer a slighly acid soil, with a pH range of 6.1 to 6.8. Unlike other western soils, which tend to be alkaline, maritime Northwest soils are usually right in this ideal rose-growing range. However, given the range of soil types, you may wish to have your soil tested. Either purchase a do-it-yourself kit at a garden center or send a sample to one of the testing facilities listed in "Sources," at the back of this book, for a more complete picture of your soil's status.

Nutrients

Of major concern to most gardeners is their soil's nutrient capacity. This can be a confusing area because of the interrelationship between water drainage, pH, and nutrient availability. If the pH is either too high or too low, nutrients in the soil may bind together in forms inaccessible to plant roots. An imbalance of nutrients or poor drainage can have a similar effect.

The major nutrients that roses take from the soil are nitrogen (N), phosphorus (P), and potassium (K). Most soils contain adequate phosphorus and potassium (in the form of potash), but nitrogen is more easily lost through water leaching or gaseous release into the air. Roses also take calcium, magnesium, sulfur, and other nutrients from the soil that must be replenished as they are used.

ADDING AMENDMENTS

Given these components of healthy soil, consider your own plot. What needs improving? Texture, drainage, pH, soil microbes, and nutrient capacity all benefit from compost or other organic matter, such as rotted manures, leaves, or green manure crops (including clover or even seaweed, a wonderfully rich source of nutrients when the salt is removed).

Specific problems can be remedied with additives. If the pH level is too low, ground agricultural lime or ammonia-based fertilizers will raise it, while also helping to break up clay and speed the decay of organic matter. If the pH level is too high, agricultural sulfur will bring it back down. First test the soil to see if the pH needs altering, then consult your local extension agent for dosages for your area.

If your soil is low in phosphorus (as it is in some coastal areas), nurseryman Scott Stiles recommends superphosphate, a form of phosphorus that has been treated to make it more water soluble. "This makes it more quickly absorbed by plant roots and faster acting." Phosphates do not move readily in soil, so they should be dug in, down to the root level, at planting time.

PROVIDING GOOD DRAINAGE

Sometimes, no matter how much you amend it, soil still will not drain sufficiently. Heavy clay subsoil or hardpan compaction is the main culprit.

One option is to rise above the problem with raised beds filled with custom-mixed soil. The poorer the drainage, the higher the beds must be built to compensate; beds 2 feet high are not too high to overcome heavy clay. According to Bob Gold, who tends over 500 roses in the middle of Seattle, "Raised beds also make it easier to care for roses, so they are ideal even in good soil conditions."

Construct raised beds from landscape timbers, bricks, blocks, or other appropriate material. Fill them in with five parts loose soil; four parts compost, rotted manure, or leaf mold; and one part sharp builder's sand (not beach sand). Add one shovelful of bonemeal or a cup of superphosphate per bush.

Another option is to install a drainage system. It means moving all the soil in the rose bed, installing drainage tile or perforated pipe, and then replacing the soil, but this may fit your plans better than raised beds or moving. Install tile or pipe 18 to 24 inches deep at an angle that slopes away from the roses.

PREPARE BEFORE PLANTING

The ideal time to prepare the soil bed for new roses is before they arrive. A late winter thaw is perfect for the occasion, but many gardeners feel the best time to plant bare-root roses in the maritime Northwest is late fall. Roots develop over winter and the plant stays dormant. Therefore, beds should be prepared in late summer. Fall-planted roses may have to be mail ordered.

Advance soil conditioning begins with removing any weeds or grass. The beauty of doing so in late winter is that there is so much less to remove. Dig a hole large enough to allow for the young roots to expand freely—2 feet by 2 feet or so. Loosen the bottom of the hole with a spading fork, then refill it with as much compost, manure, and good loose soil as you can get your hands on. Fresh manures added at this stage are all right, as they will mellow before planting time. Sprinkle in bonemeal or superphosphate, bloodmeal, greensand, or other amendments. Stir well; a spading fork makes the job of mixing easier.

Although roses can be left in their containers for several days, it is really best to get them into the ground as soon as possible after they arrive. Then there is less chance of the plants drying out and a greater chance of the roots getting off to an early start. Immediate planting also eliminates extra handling that may damage roots or canes.

Get ready for the new roses by digging the planting holes before your bring them home or receive them through the mail. Obviously, before you have the plants in hand, you can only guesstimate the size of the hole, but it is much less trouble to fill in or expand than to dig the hole after the plants arrive.

Adding to Your Collection

By considering the needs of your future roses, as well as your own expectations, you may have narrowed down your "wish list." After careful site planning and soil preparation, the varieties you choose and the individual plants you actually buy are the most critical aspects of creating a beautiful rose garden.

Shopping for Roses

As with any other consumer item, there are good ways to buy roses and not-so-good ways. Mail-order nurseries and local retail outlets have their pros and cons, as do the manner in which the roses are sold—bare root, potted, or boxed.

Mail Order

The finest roses are shipped directly from the suppliers to you at the appropriate time for planting. This cuts down significantly on the amount of time the young rose spends out of the ground and on the amount of handling it must endure. Just be sure to order early; suppliers are inundated with orders during planting season.

Local Specialty Growers

Local growers also can be a great source for roses. Deal only with retailers that guarantee their roses for at least 30 days. If you are fortunate enough to live near a producer whose roses can be viewed in the field, take advantage of the situation. You will get the best picture of how a variety grows by actually looking at it.

Stores and Nurseries

It seems that everybody gets into the rose business in the spring and local stores and nurseries will stock them temporarily. If you buy early

49

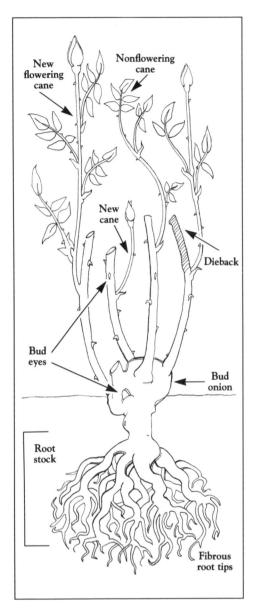

New flowering cane

Nonflowering cane

New cane

Dieback

Bud eyes

Bud onion

Root stock

Fibrous root tips

Parts of a rose in the spring.
Note the fibrous root system, planting
depth, and the open shape from pruning.

and follow the guidelines for the type of packaging, you can bring home some nice roses at a good price.

To find out where to order a specific rose, use the *Combined Rose List*, an alphabetical listing of all roses currently in retail commerce throughout the world, and suppliers. See "Sources," at the back of this book, for more information.

WAYS TO BUY ROSES

The majority of roses are sold "bare root." This means the rose has been dug up while dormant, with no soil around the roots. It has also been pruned, tagged, and sometimes packaged, as well as graded. The rest of the roses are sold potted or boxed.

Bare-root roses are offered for sale in different ways. Some experts feel that the best are heeled in sawdust. The roots are left unwrapped so that you can inspect both ends of any prospective plants. Retail nurseries offer roses with roots packaged in plastic or in paper boxes. If sold by mail order, the roots will be wrapped in plastic or foil and filled in with damp peat or sawdust. Carefully inspect any roses you are considering, whether before you buy at the nursery or after you receive a mail-order shipment. Pass by or return any that don't pass inspection.

Roses are also sold in pots, growing and usually blooming. Miniature roses are often sold this way year-round, but most often full-sized roses are offered this way later in the season.

Full-sized potted roses may have been grown in their containers, as are Miniatures, but chances are that they were once bare-root specimens that didn't sell. The nursery pots up these plants and offers them for sale during the late spring and summer. This doesn't necessarily mean that they are inferior, but do inspect them closely. Check for vigorous growth, and be wary of any twiggy growth or dieback. These are warnings that the rose has spent too much time in the container and may be seriously rootbound. Avoid any roses other than Minis that are planted in small containers. The roots may have been overpruned and may not have been kept moist while on the sales floor. Be sure to inspect both sides of the leaves for signs of pests or diseases. Close quarters and large numbers of plants create the perfect environment for these troubles to spread.

If you plan to buy prepackaged roses from a store, call first to find out when the rose shipment is due to arrive. You will not only get first pick, but also the freshest possible plants. Beware of "bargains," such as packaged roses that have sat around so long they have finally been marked down for "clearance." Although cheap, they may not have survived, especially if they have broken dormancy (and are sprouting a couple of leaves).

Packaging, and the amount of time the roses spend in it, can affect the health of the plant. Plastic is great for keeping the roots moist, but over time it can create a "greenhouse effect," which prompts the plants to break dormancy. Roses also lose moisture by evaporation through the exposed canes, so after a while dehydration is a concern.

Store displays can be bad news for plastic-wrapped roses. They are often piled up outside and left to the mercy of drying winds or sunshine and the extremes of spring temperatures. The wrapping makes it impossible to water the roots, but retailers often try to keep them moist by misting. Unfortunately, this also stimulates them to break dormancy and grow. The longer these roses wait at the store, the worse shape they will be in before you bring them home. Avoid buying plastic-wrapped roses after the end of March.

Carefully examine roses sold in paper boxes. Their roots must be pruned severely to fit into pre-sized boxes, so they face the same retail storage conditions. Their advantage over plastic-wrapped roses is the opening at the top of the box; in theory, this allows the retailer or you to add water to keep the roots moist. A sterile growing medium is packed around the roots instead of the peat and sawdust that is packed around the roots of plastic-wrapped roses. You place the box directly into the ground at planting time, which cuts down on handling.

Consider yourself the Quality Control Expert for your rose garden. Cast an unmercifully critical eye on each plant you inspect. Your mission is to introduce into your rose garden only the best individual plants of the varieties you have selected. There should be several sturdy, branching roots. Reject any that have dry-looking or spindly roots, or any that show signs of nematode infestation (nodules on roots) or illness. The canes should be firm, with green wood just beneath the surface. Withered canes show a plant has been dehydrated. The stems should have several healthy buds. Check the entire plant for signs of disease, such as discolored patches, abnormal growths, lesions, or deformities.

The best roses are graded "1." To qualify, a rose must put on the amount of cane growth appropriate for its type. For instance, Hybrid Teas or Grandifloras must produce three or four canes not less than ⅜ inch thick and at least 18 inches long prior to being pruned for market.

Once a rose has been processed and shipped, the grade is your only clue to how well it was doing before it was dug. Don't gamble on those with a grade of 2, and think twice about those graded 1½. These have already proved to be less vigorous than the premium roses graded 1 and may never catch up.

DON'T OVERSPEND

The amount you can expect to pay for roses depends on the supplier, the time of year, the variety of rose, and whether it is bare root or potted. Bare-root roses are always the better investment, cost the least, and have the best chance of surviving the shock of transplant. There are hundreds of suitable varieties available for under $12. Higher-priced roses may be new introductions that cost more because supply sometimes does not meet demand. The rarer the variety, the higher the price tag—no indication of a superior plant.

The time of year makes quite a difference in the cost of roses. As the season progresses and roses are potted up and offered for sale in containers, the extra time and investment the nursery has invested will be passed on to you. Potted roses often go for $10 to $20. One exception is Miniatures, which are most often sold in containers for prices ranging from $4 to $10 for most varieties. The other exception is grafted Tree Roses, or Standards, which may be priced as high as $50 or more. Of course, as the season moves on, the retailer will mark down old stock plants, but these bargains are not often a good buy.

IMPORT NEW VARIETIES

If your favorite outlet doesn't have the rose you want, import your own. (Find several foreign nurseries in the "Rose Buying Directory," at the back of this book.)

Interstate, or even international, rose buying is an easy way to expand your rose collection. Of course, there are a few restrictions.

Importing roses from out of state is usually as easy as picking up a catalog and dialing the phone. There are no special permits to consider. Likewise for Canadian-American sales. However, things get a bit more complicated when ordering from abroad.

Canadians who wish to import roses from overseas can do so simply by placing an order with the supplier. United States citizens wishing to do so must first apply to the Department of Agriculture for a permit. (See "Rose Buying Directory" for address.) Roses that are imported from abroad must be quarantined in your yard for a period of two years, and the USDA will send a representative to verify your quarantine area before your permit is granted. Once you are approved you will be sent a batch of tags, one of which is to be filled out and sent with each order you place abroad. The tags are good for five years. The process of obtaining a permit, quarantine inspection, and approval takes only about a month.

CREATE YOUR OWN ROSES

A truly creative alternative to shopping for roses is to propagate your own. Rose plants can be started from seed or by rooting parts of a parent plant. To start roses from seed, collect ripe seeds from mature hips in the early fall after nature has taken its course, or intervene by hand pollinating to cross specific varieties.

To root cuttings, take a 6-inch tip from a growing cane just as the flowers fade, remove all but the top two leaves. Apply rooting hormone to the cut end of the slip to speed the processes, and then push the cutting into moist sand or rooting medium. Roses with long, flexible canes can be propagated by "layering." Bring a section of cane to ground level, cover it with soil, and allow it to root. After new roots have formed, cut the cane from the parent plant and then dig up the new plant and transplant it.

CHAPTER 6

Ready to Plant

You did it. You contemplated all the qualities of the roses you wanted from color and perfume to health and vigor. You made your choices from catalogs or nursery shelves, then inspected each plant until only the finest individual specimens met your approval. You are about to grow one impressive rose garden.

The importance of immediate planting can't be overstressed. Doing so simply eliminates the myriad of things that can go wrong. But if you can't get your new roses into the ground right away, you *can* store them with little or no damage.

To store bare-root roses, simply keep them cool and moist. If the roots are allowed to dry out the plant will die. If they are kept moist but not cool enough, the plant will break dormancy and sprout delicate new growth that could easily be injured at planting time or killed by a late spring frost. To store potted roses, the rules are even more simple: Keep the roots moist.

One method of storing bare-root roses is called "healing in." Dig a trench with a slope along one side and lay the roses against the side of the trench, roots downward. Cover the plants entirely with damp soil or sand and keep them watered until planting time. But, if you can go to that much trouble, just plant them. The alternative is to pack the roots with a medium that will hold moisture, such as thoroughly wet peat, sawdust, or vermiculite, and then wrap them in wet rags or newspaper and place in a cool (not freezing) holding area. Check the roots daily to be sure they don't dry out or soak overnight.

PLANTING

Getting off to a good start is important to a plant's ability to acquire and metabolize the nutrients necessary to grow healthy foliage, strong canes, and bushels of blossoms. Bare-root roses can be planted any time after the ground has thawed enough to be worked, provided the day-time temperatures are at least 40 °F. This is usually between January and March in the Northwest.

Don't plant on windy or unusually cold days, to avoid stressing the plant. Roses planted after the end of March may not establish them-selves well until the following year. Potted roses can be planted until the middle of summer, after which it becomes more difficult for them to establish themselves.

Roses can also be planted or transplanted in this region as soon as they go dormant in the fall. Some gardeners feel this gives the roots the best possible start in the spring.

Bare-Root Roses

To plant a bare-root rose, first fill a large bucket with enough warm water to thoroughly cover the roots. Immerse and let it soak for at least an hour to overnight. The idea is for the roots to absorb as much water as possible. Don't overdo it, though, as prolonged (more than 12 hours) oxygen deprivation can kill the roots.

You may want to add rooting hormone to the soaking bath, according to the horticultural newsletter *Hortideas*. The hormone stim-ulates root production, which aids significantly in getting the rose established. The only drawback is that the plant will not grow as vig-orously above ground during the first year of growth as it would have if left untreated. This is because the plant has been manipulated into putting all its energy into root production. In following years, however, the plant will benefit from the superior foundation it has put down. The trade-off is between the instant gratification of seeing new roses grow and bloom in their first year, and the long-term benefit of well-rooted, established roses.

The next step is to prepare the dormant plant for its awakening into the world. Check for any broken or dead roots and snip them off. Trim long roots back to 8 to 10 inches to encourage the plant to send out a new wave of hair roots. It is much more beneficial to inspire new root growth than to try and cram every existing odd-shaped one into the planting hole.

Cut back the canes to encourage new growth and to minimize the surface area of the plant vulnerable to dehydration. The less topgrowth the roots have to support, the more quickly they will become estab-lished. (See Chapter 9 on pruning for tips on placing the cuts.) Cut out any dead or puny canes flush to the bud union on grafted roses, or to the main stalk on own-rooted roses. Do not cut into the bud union.

Trim any broken canes with a clean cut to prevent diseases from finding an entry point. Most prepackaged roses have already been pruned back for planting, but a light repruning helps to wake them up. The result should be a well-balanced plant, with open, spreading roots and two to four canes that spread away from an open center.

Place the rose in the hole, holding on to the base of the canes, and check the hole for size. Make any necessary adjustments in size and shape. Sprinkle a couple of handfuls of bonemeal (or a cup of super-phosphate) in the bottom of the hole, backfill partially with dirt from the hole, then mound the dirt up inside the hole into a little cone. This cone will support the rose's roots while you fill in the hole. You may have to mound the dirt, check the position of the plant, and then mound some more before you get it just right. The level at which roses should be planted causes as much debate as religion and politics. Own-rooted roses can be planted at the same depth as, or slightly lower than, they were originally grown.

It is with grafted roses that the controversy arises. The long-standing rule for the north Pacific coast has been to plant with the bud union 1 to 2 inches above the soil line. Many believe that exposure to sunlight increases the productivity of the graft, causing it to produce more flowering shoots. "I don't know about that," counters Rich Baer of the Portland Rose Society. "Look at people in places like Minnesota, where the only way they can grow hybrids is to sink the bud union several inches below the soil. Roses still bloom there."

Since hundreds of Northwest rose lovers lost thousands of roses during the sudden cold snap of the winter of 1990–91, Baer has been advising to plant with the bud union 2 inches below the soil line. Not only does this provide extra protection from winter cold, but it also gives the grafted variety an opportunity to establish its own root system. On its own roots, even if the plant freezes to the ground, it may survive the winter.

The best compromise is to plant new roses with the top of the bud union just showing above the soil line. Rose gardener Scott Johns feels that "this way the graft can still receive sunlight, but the soil contact gives it a chance to send down its own roots."

Once the rose is positioned over the soil mound, spread the roots out evenly around it and gently refill the hole about two-thirds full.

Keep checking the roots and placement of the plant as you go. Gently press the soil down by hand to force out any air pockets, then fill the partially filled-in hole with water. As it drains it will filter soil down. Finish filling the hole after the water drains and water deeply one more time. Mound soil or mulch up over the canes until only the top 1 inch or so peaks out. This will help protect the plant from extreme temperature changes and drying winds.

"The number one killer of new roses," warns Rich Baer, "is dehydration. If you can't cover the entire plant with soil, fit a paper grocery bag over the top and anchor it with as much soil as possible to help hold in the humidity."

As the rose begins to awaken, around the first of May, carefully begin to take off the mounded soil or mulch, a little at a time. The first shoots will be yellow instead of green or red, but they will take on their normal color as soon as they get a good dose of sunshine.

Boxed Roses

Boxed roses were designed to be easy to plant. They can go into the ground while still dormant or when growing. The box will have specific instructions for planting, but be sure to cut a few slits in the sides to give the roots an easy escape route. Although the box material will eventually degrade, the sooner the roots can penetrate the soil the better. Don't add water to the contents of the box before the hole is filled with soil or the medium will run out through the slits.

Potted Roses

Bear in mind when planting a potted rose that it is actively growing, so extra care must be taken not to injure tender growth.

Water the dirt in the pot well before planting and do not remove the rose until you are ready to transfer it to the hole. Dig the hole and place the potted rose inside to check for planting depth. When ready to plant, remove the container. Do so very carefully so as not to disturb the roots. Metal or heavy plastic containers should be cut away with tin snips, not yanked off. Otherwise, hold the container sideways and gently tap to loosen the root ball. If you must tug on the rose, do so very gently. Once it is free of the pot, loosen the surface roots from the soil ball. This will encourage them to grow outward. Carefully place the plant in the hole, while supporting the soil ball. Check for depth, then proceed as before.

HELP YOUR ROSES GET ESTABLISHED

If you amended the soil before planting, there is no need to fertilize new plants in their first year. In fact, chemical fertilizers often burn tender new roots. In its first few weeks, the plant will send out roots to support itself.

What the newly planted rose needs now is water and plenty of it. Lack of sufficient water is one of the main reasons new roses fail. A light foliar feeding of fish emulsion, manure tea, or a low dose of synthetic food (as directed on the label) will give young plants a midsummer boost.

Though of no concern to the roses, there is another step that is very helpful to the rose gardener, that of labeling the different varieties. Many come with tags attached. These should be removed so they don't tighten and constrict the canes as the plants grow. There are many elegant rose markers available, or you can make your own. It is also a good idea, when growing many roses, to map out the garden as the roses go into the ground. Then you will always know what grows where.

TRANSPLANTING

Just as you have gotten everything into place and have drawn up and filled in a sophisticated map of the garden, something doesn't look quite right. That's it—that orange-blooming rose is clashing with the pinkish purple of that clematis. The rose goes.

Not to worry, the odds are good that your rose can happily survive transplanting to a new location. Unless the rose has been in place for years, it should take no more than a season or two for it to recover from the move. But there is a significant amount of transplant shock, so the rose should be pampered accordingly at first.

First prepare the soil and the planting hole as you would for a new rose. Treat the transplant either as you would a potted rose, with the root ball intact, or as a bare-root rose, in which case you wash the soil away from the roots and prune them back. In either case, only move the roses when they are fully dormant, usually from the end of December through the first of March.

Begin by thoroughly saturating the ground around the transplant-to-be with water. This will loosen the soil and saturate the roots. Dig a circle around the plant about 18 inches wide and as deep. If treating the rose as a potted plant, dig out one side and slip a piece of burlap into the hole. As you continue to dig out the rose, edge the fabric around and under the root ball to hold it together. Lift by the fabric and transfer to the new hole. If it must be transported any distance, wet the burlap well and tie it up around the roots.

To transplant a rose as if it were a bare-root plant, dig it out as before, then wash the soil from the roots. Trim the roots as for a newly purchased bare-root rose and proceed to plant in the same way.

After the rose has been replanted, prune it back to remove at least the top half of the plant. This will decrease the burden on the roots and hopefully some of the transplant shock.

One problem you may encounter, especially when attempting to transplant an older, well-established rose, is "the rose that won't die." Old Garden Roses that have sent their own suckering roots down and out through the soil for years are tough and determined. Many is the surprised farmer who, having yanked an old tangled mass of canes from the earth with a team of horses or a tractor, finds familiar new shoots sprouting from the same ground the following spring. You may have to resort to chemical herbicides if a repeat pulling doesn't discourage the plant.

Once you have your roses snugly tucked into their permanent beds, you can sit back and admire them. For roses to really shine, however, they need to know you love them. Talk to them if you like, but actions speak louder than words. Their requirements are few and simple, as you will see in the next chapter. Tend to them loyally, and they will provide you with ample rewards.

CHAPTER 7

Tending North Coast Roses

"Tending the rose garden." Such ethereal images those words convey. Long, lazy afternoons spent strolling amongst the color-splashed, scent-burdened canes. You could just while away the hours doting over your roses. Or does your life run a little short of long, lazy, rose-doting afternoons? Many of us barely find time to turn on the sprinkler. Chances are, the time you have to devote to your roses falls somewhere in between.

JUST ADD WATER

Sufficient water is a basic necessity for healthy roses. They need it to help take up nutrients from the soil, to carry on cellular metabolism, and to give their bodies shape and substance. Thirsty roses fail to thrive, become susceptible to opportunistic pests and diseases, and produce dry, papery leaves and few, if any, flowers. Wet feet, too, are bad news for the majority of roses. Waterlogged soil deprives the roots of oxygen; the rose cannot carry on its necessary metabolic functions and eventually will die.

Sufficient watering depends on the circumstances. Roses lose water through evaporation via leaf pores, other surface areas, and soil runoff. In hot, dry weather evaporation increases dramatically, from both the plant and the soil. Wind robs moisture from all surface areas. And loose, sandy soils allow water to run through before the roots can absorb it. On the other hand, poorly drained clay holds water so well that the plant roots may suffocate. So how much is enough?

Most roses in average maritime Northwest growing conditions require from 2 to 3 inches of water per week during the growing season for optimal growth. If drainage is good, it is almost impossible to overwater. Summer temperatures above 85°F or winds increase the demand.

How the water is supplied is almost as critical as the amount. Rain will provide much of it during the spring and fall. As the season becomes drier, you must supplement the water supply. When irrigating, water roses deeply. Soak the soil to a depth of 16 inches or more every 10 to 14 days. Deep watering is best because it causes the roots to search deeper for moisture, a saving grace in our all-too-familiar times of drought. If only the top few inches of soil is moistened, then that is where the roots will grow. Then along comes a heat wave. Surface roots dry out quickly, which stresses the plant and affects growth, flowering, and overall health. As tough and adaptable as roses are, you still have to give them a fair chance.

To determine whether your roses are getting their due, water as usual, then carefully dig down near the roots. If the soil isn't wet 16 inches down, let the water run longer from now on. A long, cool drink will tide most roses over for about two weeks. Rain or cool temperatures will extend this time; hot or windy conditions will shorten it by as much as half or more. Continue to water until the roses begin to go dormant, indicated by blossoms falling and leaves turning color or dropping, depending upon type.

Several strategies exist to water roses, and lots of expensive equipment is sold to get the job done. The best method is through drip irrigation, which can be as unsophisticated as turning the garden hose on to a trickle and forgetting about it for a while, or as fancy as an in-ground system. Drip irrigation releases water slowly so that it is absorbed by the soil, with the least amount of loss through evaporation.

Prize-winning rosarian Bob Gold recommends a low spray of no more than 2 to 3 inches high that saturates all ground, soaks in fertilizers, and doesn't get foliage wet (yet discourages spider mites). PVC pipe and Dramm nozzles can be used to create his ideal system.

If you really want a hot debate, forget politics and bring up overhead sprinklers at a garden club meeting. Many use them and many shake their heads at those who do. Overhead sprinklers were designed for even water distribution over a lawn, not to reach the roots of roses. One of the major drawbacks is that of wasting water. On a hot or windy day, more water is lost into the air than reaches the waiting roots; overhead watering is also a great way to spread moisture-loving diseases. Fungi splash from leaf to leaf and plant to plant with the spraying water. If you use organic pesticides, the spray washes them away, which means you have to re-apply them. The good news is that a regular sprinkling helps to remove dust and environmental residues, and in hot weather a good splash of cold water greatly disturbs and diminishes spider mite populations, a significant pest in the region. Some argue that regular overhead sprinkling prevents fungi and bacteria from invading the plant by washing them away. If overhead sprinklers are your only choice, turn them on early in the morning and off by midday so that the foliage can dry.

The greatest demand for water is when the roses are newly planted. The other peak demand is during hot, dry weather. Naturally, nothing inspires thirst more than a water shortage. But there are ways to cope. A thick mulch is a great line of defense against moisture loss.

Once the butt of rain and rowboat jokes, cities from Vancouver, B.C., south have been forced to economize on their water supplies. Water rationing and irrigation bans have occurred in heavily populated areas due to drought.

Under drought and rationing conditions, water management becomes a challenge. Some rose lovers throughout the region bury a vertical pipe 2 feet deep to water roses so that all water is delivered directly to deep roots. Others siphon out and recycle bath water (use only mild, biodegradable soap). Still others save water for their roses by water-wise strategies, such as less toilet flushing and laundry washing. Several gardeners reported that they begin facing summer in the winter by collecting rainwater for later use on their plants. We are nothing if not resourceful in the name of our roses.

If all else fails, remember that most roses are surprisingly tough and seem to have a true will to live. If they have been well watered throughout the spring and early summer, they should be able to take a dry spell in stride. The roots will have "learned" to look downward for water. When drought strikes, it is actually better not to water roses at all for a while than to "teach" them to send the roots back towards the parched surface by dribbling too little water on them now and then.

Some varieties are more drought tolerant than others. Species Roses, many Rugosas, and the tough Rugosa hybrids are notable for adapting to the dry garden. Some modern Shrubs, such as the Kordes Shrub 'Frühlingsgold', are good for that area out of reach of a hose. Many Old Garden Roses are perfectly up to the modern water challenges because they evolved in a time and place where water was plentiful until the early summer. They remain among the better choices for drought-afflicted areas. Roses need adequate water to perform well, but they are forgiving of temporary lapses.

Difficult though it may be under average conditions, a rose can have too much water. The problem is usually due to poor drainage. If poor soil structure or subsoil hardpan is to blame, see Chapter 4 for ideas. Consider planting varieties that naturally tolerate soggy soils. The Species Roses *Rosa gymnocarpa*, *R. carolina*, and *R. nitida* are among the more flood forgiving.

PROVIDE PROPER NUTRIENTS

Roses can obtain nutrients from chemical fertilizers or organic sources. But the consequences of the two methods are different. Chemical fertilizers are formulated to be water soluble, which makes them instantly available to plant roots. This is why they are faster acting. Unfortunately, they can burn plants or leach out through soil and into groundwater. Lastly, a handful of chemicals once in a while will do nothing to build up the healthy soil needed by plants. However, they can have a significant impact on pH levels.

Fresh manures are high in nitrogen, so should not be applied directly to the rose, as the plant may be injured. Plant roots absorb nitrogen very quickly, and if too much is consumed it forms salts inside the plant, which burns the tissues. Aged manures have burned off excess nitrogen. If you want to take full advantage of the nutrients in fresh manure, use it to make compost. A balanced compost can fulfill all your roses' nutritional needs. It builds the soil, releases nutrients slowly so that the plants can metabolize them, and has no negative impact whatsoever.

Of course, organic fertilizers are also available commercially, as is a range of synthetics. Many are formulated especially for roses. Read package labels for feeding directions. They may suggest feeding via the roots, as with compost, or foliar feeding, where the product is dissolved in water and sprayed onto the leaves. When using granules, be sure to soak the ground before applying to ensure uptake. Always follow the product labels and never overfeed.

Foliar feeding acts as a quick pick-me-up to hungry roses. Since the nutrients are absorbed through the leaves they are readily available to the plant to use "on site." Don't apply on days when the temperature is over 85°F or when the wind is blowing. Make your own foliar manure tea by soaking a cheesecloth bag filled with fresh manure or compost overnight in a bucket or barrel of warm water. One pound of manure per 2 gallons of water makes a good ratio. Spray on foliage or douse the roots.

Feeding frequency depends on the type of rose, the soil, and what's on the menu. Roses that bloom only once a year, such as Species Roses and most Old Garden Roses and Ramblers, will thrive on one hearty meal in the early spring. A good serving of compost will tide them over for the year.

Repeat bloomers use up a lot of energy and benefit from a few foliar "snacks" just prior to each flush of flowers. Weekly or biweekly is even better but it takes more effort. If using chemical fertilizers, plan on feeding about once a month during the blooming season, then stop feeding in August to avoid promoting new growth late in the season that may not survive the first frosts.

The type of soil determines how long commercial fertilizers stay in the vicinity of the plant's roots. They will filter through sandy soils quickly and need to be applied more frequently. Experience will help you to determine whether your roses are being fed adequately. Healthy roses flower freely according to their variety, produce deep, true colors, and have healthy green foliage and canes. Their good health makes them less likely to be attacked by pests or diseases.

Deficiencies or excesses in the diet take time to show up, but many have telltale indicators. For instance, iron deficiency is not unusual, though it is rarely attributed to a lack of iron in the soil. The cause is more likely to be poor drainage or a high (alkaline) pH level. For help, apply iron as a foliar spray to plants exhibiting the hallmark signs of yellow leaves with green veins. The best solution, however, is to correct the underlying problem. Chelated iron also helps bring out blue tones in roses such as 'Reine de Violettes'.

WEED AND CULTIVATE

Weeds sink deep roots into the soil to compete with roses for water. Then they spread out more roots to choke out those of the roses, in addition to using up nutrients. Weeds make poor rosebed-fellows, not only because of their scruffy appearance, but because of their use of food and water.

There are several approaches to eliminating weeds from the rose beds. For many, the simplest way is to rummage around on all fours in hand-to-weed combat or to use scuffle hoes that scrape the surface to uproot weeds.

Use herbicides with care in the rose garden. The Portland International Rose Test Garden uses pre-emergent herbicides, those that attack weeds in the seeds and seedling stages. A big benefit to this type of spray is that much less is needed. Once the weeds get up and growing it takes a bigger dose to do them in.

Some herbicides work by contact, killing any part of the plant they touch. Others work systemically, as they are taken up through the roots and kill the entire plant. Contact herbicides are effective on grass; broadleaf weeds, such as dandelions, succumb more readily to systemics.

Never spray on a windy day, as the poisons may drift into the roses. Also, never use the same sprayer for herbicides that you use for anything that is sprayed directly onto the roses, such as pesticides, fungicides, or foliar food. Even a trace of residue can harm a rose. Since the risk is greater near tinier plants, don't use herbicides around Miniatures. Finally, as with any other type of poison, read and follow all label directions carefully, and clean up thoroughly afterwards. You should also be aware that herbicides contribute to groundwater contamination.

Cultivate around roses to about a couple of inches deep. Along with the benefits of loosening soil for better water drainage, incorporating organic matter, and disturbing germinating weeds or soil-borne pests, thorough cultivating gets you into close contact with your plants so that you can inspect them. And if by chance you sever an occasional root, don't worry.

No matter which strategy you use, begin early in the spring. Young weeds are much more tender than mature ones. The roots don't penetrate as far, which makes them easier to remove and less likely to regenerate. Tender spring growth is also more susceptible to sprays and dies back more quickly and completely.

MULCH

Would you like to get in on a simple secret that would make all the last three chores—watering, feeding, and weeding—easier and more efficient? A thick layer of mulch will preserve precious moisture. Some materials break down to release a steady supply of nutrients that

Mulches

COMPOST: Rich, attractive color. Highest food value.

BARK MULCH (SHREDDED OR FINE CHIPS, NOT CHUNKS):
Very attractive. Degrades slowly. Low in nitrogen but very high in organic matter.

SHREDDED LEAVES: High in organic matter and nutrients.

LAWN CLIPPINGS: High in organic matter and nutrition but not the most attractive. Rake into rows and dry thoroughly or they will mat. May be used as a bottom layer. Don't use clippings from lawns that are chemically treated.

MANURE: Must be aged or the high concentration of salts will burn the plants. Not bad looking if processed through a shredder.

STRAW: Straw, not hay. Hay is loaded with ripe seeds. Straw is high in humus and potassium, but the carbohydrate content is so high it uses up a lot of nitrogen as it degrades.

NEWSPAPER: Effective against weeds. The paper breaks down into organic matter and the ink supplies trace elements. Looks awful, so cover with a layer of soil, bark mulch, rocks, etc.

SAWDUST OR SHAVINGS: Best if composted. Decomposes very slowly and, if worked into the soil, uses up a lot of nitrogen.

ROCKS OR GRAVEL: Lasts forever, but few benefits. No nutrient or organic content, lets weeds through if not thick enough, and radiates heat in hot weather.

provides a slow-release self-feeding program. And, buried beneath a carpet of mulch, weeds suffocate before they have a chance. Mulching also helps to protect surface roots from temperature fluctuations.

The north Pacific coast is blessed with some truly fine materials to use as mulch, bark dust being one of the best. Compost and shredded leaves are also excellent choices.

Wait until the soil has warmed to apply mulch. If you had applied winter protection, then remove it first. Be sure that any weeds that have surfaced are pulled; by getting an early start you may beat the weeds to the deed entirely. Water the roses deeply, then mulch.

A 2- to 6-inch layer of any of the materials listed in the box on page 67 will protect full-sized roses; Minis need only an inch or two. Every inch you spread now will save you work and water in the future. Each year, replenish degrading mulches, those that add to the soil. Such mulches may need a second application during the summer. Don't use anything with active weed or grass seeds.

WEATHERIZE

Sturdy and determined as they are, at times roses need a little protection from the elements. Wind, sun, frost, and rainy days may all take their toll.

FROST AND COLD There is no doubt that extreme cold, especially coupled with thawing spells, stresses roses. The debate begins with what you should do about it. In coastal areas, frost protection is usually not worth discussing. Few roses, except for very tender varieties, suffer damage. For those in the shadow of the mountains, however, winters can be much colder. Still, few roses suffer damage.

Prepare for the ravages of winter in the summer. Well-watered, healthy roses have all the advantages. Stop feeding roses by the end of August to avoid prompting new growth that could be killed by an early freeze. Cutting back on the watering after the end of summer encourages the plant to harden off.

As the season ends, leave any spent flowers on the bush. This will encourage the plant to set fruit, another natural signal that it is time to get ready for winter.

Mound a heavy layer of mulch or a foot or more of soil at the base of the plant to help protect it. Use the soil from elsewhere in the garden instead of mounding it up from the base of the plant. This uncovers more roots than it covers.

Tree Roses and Climbers need help if the temperature drops below 10°F (see Chapter 2). During the winter of 1990–91 the Portland Rose Garden lost its tree roses due to the extreme and sudden cold. "It's the unpredictability of normally mild weather that is murder to roses," notes park attendant Rodney Pratt. Serious protection calls for carefully uprooting one side of the plant and tipping it onto the ground. It can then be anchored down and covered with several inches of soil. After the danger of heavy frost has passed the rose can be excavated.

If an early spring thaw tricks your roses into a false start, prune the canes back to any buds that have not yet begun to swell, to prevent dieback of any shoots that sprout too early (see Chapter 9).

Problems can also arise if the winter isn't cold enough. Being native only to the northern hemisphere, many varieties require a winter chill in order to grow and flower the following season. If some canes remain bare, prune them out and wait till next season. Lack of sufficiently cool temperatures is a common problem with Miniatures that are indoors. "These roses must have a cool-temperature rest period in order to grow and bloom," says King County extension agent George Pinyuh (on a prerecorded tape accessed by phone). "Keep them outdoors in a protected area for 45 to 60 days, then bring them in and repot them." If left out in the cold during November and December, they can be brought in to bloom in January, provided they are given supplementary (fluorescent) light. From 16 to 18 hours of light daily is recommended. If you can't provide this, simply leave them in the garden to follow their natural seasons.

Another potential problem is when plants retain their leaves into the winter. As the leaves decay on the bush, any diseases also rapidly multiply. In late fall, strip the leaves and clean up the bed. Cut bushes back a little at this time to minimize wind-rocking damage to roots.

RAIN, RAIN Cool, wet weather seems to bother roses as much as it does people. They go into a slump. Without lots of sunshine, they don't bloom well. Constantly damp leaves are very susceptible to fungal diseases that thrive in such conditions. Cool, overcast days may cause a condition known as balling, where the flowers fail to open completely. Cull these doomed blooms and wait for better weather. Roses with fewer petals are less likely to come down with this malady and are a wise choice for places where the summers are cool or foggy.

You can't make it stop raining. The best insurance you can give your roses is to prune them into an open bush, with lots of air circulation, as described in Chapter 9.

CHAPTER 8

How to Solve Problems

We are not the only rose admirers. From bugs to bacteria to trophy-sized deer, the rose must fend off a bevy of beasts.

TO SPRAY OR NOT TO SPRAY

The philosophy of pest and disease control in roses runs the gamut of extremes. There are organic purists who take advantage of resistant varieties and cultural methods, never spray a rose, and have a bounty of beautiful blooms to show for it. Others, believing prevention is the key, are devoted to a spray program that stops disease before damage is done. In between are those who spray some plants and not others, or who spray only after a problem is evident.

"A dormant oil/lime sulfur spray will prevent many pests and diseases," advises Raintree's Scott Stiles, "and it's very safe." He also recommends insecticidal soap or rotenone on an as-needed basis for pests.

If you decide to use chemical sprays, don't spray on windy, rainy, or hot days. *Do* be sure to coat both sides of the leaf and to thoroughly clean up when finished. There are many different products for the control of pests and diseases, some in combinations. Systemic fungicides and pesticides are effective, but those that are applied to the soil can contaminate groundwater. Be savvy and be safe.

ARS rosarian Bob Gold uses chemicals carefully for his 500 roses. He sprays weekly with a fungicide but only sprays pests with insecticides or miticides as needed. He notes that more-potent systemic fungicides are coming on the market.

PESTS

Aphids or plant lice love cool, wet weather. One of the most common of rose pests, they congregate in the most tender new growth, often obliterating new flower buds.

Several species abound, in shades from light green to brown. They are tiny, tear-shaped, soft-bodied insects, some with wings. Control them easily with harmless methods, such as blasting them with cold water from the hose, soaking them with insecticidal soap, or allowing ladybugs or lacewings to eat their fill. Hot weather reduces their numbers.

Cane borers are sneaky little insects that burrow through cut ends of canes. Though elusive and seldom seen themselves, the damage they cause is all-too-often evident in the tops of canes that die back due to their work. Thwart cane borers by painting over pruning cuts with a pruning wound sealant.

Deer find roses to be a special favorite. They can wipe out a bush in one meal, so discourage them. Since they are most active at dusk and daybreak, rural and suburban gardeners may wish to cover their roses for the evening with a crop cover or netting. ARS meetings cover this topic frequently.

Gall wasps are tiny and stingless but they make their homes in odd-looking growths. The conspicuous growths do not damage the plant, other than affecting its looks.

Gall wasps common to *Rosa nutkana* form a spindle-shaped growth that looks like a giant rose hip. Other galls, such as those that prefer *R. eglanteria*, are mossy-looking masses built between the canes. These can be cut out if unsightly.

Leafhoppers are small, greenish yellow insects that feed on the undersides of leaves, causing mottled patches and white stippling on foliage. They are too fast to hand pick but you can battle them with insecticidal soap.

Mites take over as aphids subside in hot weather. They infiltrate the underworld (of leaves) with fine, gossamer webs. You may only be able to see specks, but look for telltale signs of yellowed leaves, often sprinkled with brown dots caused by their feeding habits. Mites are related to spiders and bear a striking resemblance if you can see that well. Individuals live only a few days, but populations escalate quickly during periods of hot, dry weather. Discourage them by keeping roses well watered and turning the sprinklers on them when they appear. Natural predators may take care of the problem if allowed.

Nematodes are microscopic soil-borne pests that adhere to the roots of roses and other plants. They prevent the roots from drawing up adequate nutrients. Avoid planting in infested soil whenever possible;

mostly sandy soil is a problem. To starve out nematodes, leave the infested area bare for two years; mulch if you want to hide the bald spots. Biological controls are available in the form of beneficial nematodes or Clandosan, a soil amendment.

Rose scale insects appear as crusty flakes on older canes and stems. They suck juices from plant tissues. The best remedies are preventive. Apply a dormant oil spray to smother overwintering scale, and if infestations persist until fall, prune out affected canes.

Rose slugs and **caterpillars** are, respectively, the larval forms of sawflies and butterflies that creep along the surface of leaves chewing large holes. Most can be controlled with pyrethrins or rotenone. *Bacillus thuringiensis* is effective against caterpillars.

Spittle bugs are little, wedge-shaped bugs that are hardly noticeable until they leave their trademark. They surround themselves in spit bubbles and suck the juices out of plant stems. These insects do no real harm to roses other than spoiling the image. Squirt them with the garden hose—go ahead, they deserve it. If you did what these guys do in public you would probably get the same treatment.

Thrips love the cool and damp, and also crave the darkness. They slip through the folds of unopened blossoms, foraging as they go. They steal the splendor from the rose, for when blossoms open they are chewed with brown spots.

Thrips are very tiny, dark colored, slender insects that scurry from sight if you investigate the petals for them. Their damage tends to be less noticable once hot weather sets in. They are tough to battle, but systemic pesticides are effective because they poison the critter through its rose petal meals.

DISEASES

Blackspot is the scourge of north Pacific coastal rose lovers. This dreaded fungal disease begins as small, dark spots on an otherwise green leaf. As it progresses, watch the spots grow and become surrounded by yellow until the entire leaf dies and falls. Severe cases can defoliate a plant and spread quickly to other roses.

Blackspot, like all fungal rose diseases, flourishes in dampness. It is caused by spores that come from previously infected leaves. It usually infects leaves lowest on the plant first, then works its way up the bush. Some roses (especially yellows that trace back to *Rosa foetida*) are very susceptible, while others vary in tolerance from resistant to virtual immunity. Consider the following steps to ban this burden from your blooms: Choose from the many blackspot-resistant rose varieties. Protect those that are less tolerant through good cultural practices. Keep the bushes pruned to an open shape to promote good air circulation. Avoid using overhead sprinklers late in the day. Pick heavily infested leaves and any that drop, and then burn them. Work on infected plants last and wash your hands well afterwards. Apply fresh mulch in the fall to smother any surviving spores. If you prefer a spray program, apply a fungicide weekly from the bottom of the plant up, including sides of leaves and ground around the plant, in addition to the above steps.

An old remedy that is receiving new attention is to spray leaves with soda water. Dissolve 1 teaspoon of baking soda in 1 gallon of water and spray both sides of the leaves. The logic is that the soda alters the pH level of the leaf surface, making it unappealing to the fungi.

Cankers are brownish spots that first appear on dead wood, then spread to infect live tissue. They are unsightly and stressful to the plant. They are also a sign that your pruning practices are lagging. Avoid cankers by pruning out dead wood before the fungus can get started. Burn the cuttings or include them in a hot compost pile.

Crown gall may at first by hard to detect, especially if only the roots are affected. The plant will be less vigorous than it should be, but this is a hard thing to compare. If the gall reaches the bud union, or crown, it will be obvious.

Gall bacteria are present in most soils. They enter a rose through a physical injury, such as a jaggedly pruned root or insect damage. This is manifested as grotesque, lumpy growths on the roots or around the crown. Whether or not it stresses the plant is debatable, but it is pervasive and ugly. A safe biological preventative, the bacterium *Agrobacterium radiobacter,* is now available. Follow directions on the label to soak roots in a solution of the bacteria and water before they are planted. Roses so treated are not afflicted.

If gall is present on your bushes, you may wish to remove them or let them stay, depending on their relative health. They are not at risk of infecting other plants because the disease is soil borne and already present. However, if you do keep any afflicted plants, be especially careful when pruning to avoid introducing the bacteria to healthy roses. Prune infected roses last, and disinfect pruning shears by soaking them in a bleach solution or other disinfectant.

Powdery mildew is easy to recognize as a dusty, white coating on new leaves and flower buds. This fungus is most common when nights are cool and days are humid. It is also a classic indication that the plant is not receiving enough water. Water-stressed plants, as well as those with a natural susceptibility, are the prime targets of this disease. Use the same steps taken to prevent blackspot. For those who use systemic fungicides, follow a spray program.

Rust appears on the underside of leaves as small orange bumps, sometimes interspersed with black. The tops of infected leaves are characteristically yellowed, but it is the flip side that completes the diagnosis. Like other fungal infections, it is spread via spores from previously infected leaves. Like the others, rust thrives in moist conditions. It is not as prevalent after cold winters. Look for naturally resistant varieties and follow the recommendations made for blackspot.

Viruses on roses may leave peculiar mottled green, yellow, or orange patterns on the leaves. Or they may show a mosaic pattern of yellow shapes, outlined in green. Other viral infections prevent the bush from flowering and may cause leaves to drop. An infected rose cannot be treated. It is possible for insects to spread the disease, so the sick rose must go. Dig it out and burn it.

If a new rose shows signs of infection it very likely was infected at the nursery, because the most common method of transmission is through tissue-to-tissue contact, such as budding. A reputable supplier will exchange an infected rose.

The demands of the rose are really quite simple. A good location, water, and food are the necessities of life. But there is one more step you must take for roses to bloom their best—that of pruning. Pruning and cutting flowers are simple processes explained in the next chapter.

Pruning and Harvesting

CHAPTER 9

Pruning is the process of removing unwanted growth. The effect it has on the rose depends on when and how it is carried out. The intent is to encourage healthy new flowering growth in a pleasing shape, but the results depend on your technique.

WHEN TO PRUNE

Timing is everything, but knowing what type of rose you have is equally important. Prune modern roses, such as Shrubs, Hybrid Musks, Hybrid Teas, Grandifloras, Floribundas, Minis, and Tree Roses grafted from any of these, just before they break dormancy, in late January through February. The process stimulates growth.

Old Garden Roses, Ramblers, and once-flowering Climbers produce their flowers on year-old wood, so don't cut them back in the early spring or you will remove the only part of the plant that can flower. Prune any once-flowering varieties only after they have bloomed for the season. They will continue to produce new growth, and it will flower the following year.

In areas with routinely high winter winds, prune in the fall to stabilize the plants. Heavy gusts through high canes toss the plant about, which can damage and loosen the roots. If winds or ice threaten your roses, cut the canes back by as much as a third.

Summertime pruning consist mainly of dead-heading and collecting bouquets. Suckers can be pulled and any dead or diseased wood or leaves should be removed.

GETTING RESULTS YOU WANT

How much growth you remove depends on the type of rose, the form you are aiming for, and whether or not you want lots of flowers or a few outstanding blossoms.

75

Light pruning is the removal of less than one-third of the total growth of the plant. This technique produces the greatest numbers of blossoms. Species Roses, Old Garden Roses, Shrubs, and Floribundas are routinely pruned this way and many Hybrid Tea enthusiasts prefer it. A few, such as 'Scarlet Meidiland' and some Minis, will thrive on almost no pruning at all.

Moderate pruning consists of removing all but the best five to eight canes and cutting these back to 18 to 24 inches. It is commonly practiced on Hybrid Teas and Grandifloras after their first year in the ground.

Reserve severe pruning for weak plants or those used to produce cut flowers. Cut back the plant to three or four canes and leave them from 6 to 10 inches long. This stimulates weak plants to produce more vigorous growth. Rose exhibitors use this method to achieve their grand blooms.

"The biggest mistake people make when pruning roses," says Dan Hinkley of Heronswood Nursery, "is not pruning enough. Removing old growth is what stimulates the rose to keep producing." Indeed, the blossoms of many modern hybrids will steadily decline if the plant is not cut back on a yearly basis. Older varieties and modern shrubs will usually do fine if only dead or diseased wood is removed. However, as much as two-thirds of the growth can be cut away without harming the plant.

Establish a yearly pruning routine for your roses. Mark the job on your calendar in advance and set aside a day to get it done.

It is also good practice to monitor the buds after you have pruned. If a bud sprouts more than one shoot, pinch out all but the strongest one. Roses grown for cutting will produce one superior blossom per stem if they are disbudded. For Floribundas, reverse the procedure by pinching out the center bud and allowing the other buds to form "sprays" of many flowers.

RECLAIMING NEGLECTED ROSES

Perhaps you've had the luck to inherit an older rose plant that has not been pruned in quite a while and is showing signs of neglect. There is an alternative to removing it that is often successful.

The first year: Cut out all dead, damaged, diseased and spindly wood. Remove any suckers. Cut back twiggy stems from remaining shoots and shorten strong side-shoots to about 6 inches. Mulch well with compost. The second year: Cut all remaining old wood back to the base of the plant. Shorten side-shoots on new growth to 6 inches. Mulch with compost. In subsequent years prune per the variety.

The 10 Commandments of Pruning

The range of growth and flowering habits among roses mandates slightly different methods, but these are the basics.

1. Use sharp tools. A dull blade will not make a clean cut, and jagged cuts lead to dieback. Use hand-held pruning shears for small canes and long-handled loppers for thicker branches. Thick deadwood needs a curved, fine-toothed handsaw, as do hard-to-reach places. Do not use anvil cutters, which crush stems. Paint large or uneven cuts with a pruning compound.

2. Wear gloves.

3. Prune judiciously. The more growth you remove, the less foliage remains to feed the plant. When in doubt, prune lightly. Severely pruned roses produce fewer flowers, but since the plant has more energy to devote to each blossom they are all the more spectacular. Less pruning means more flowers on the plant.

4. Always cut down to healthy wood. If the outer layers are green and healthy but the core, or pith, is brown or soft, make a new cut a little further down the cane. Roses that freely produce new shoots from the base of the plant, such as Centifolias and Moss Roses, should have several canes cut back to ground level to encourage this new growth. Those that produce few shoots from the base, such as Gallicas, should have only one or two shoots pruned back to the base.

5. Remove dead wood first, then the diseased or weak growth. Cut such wood flush to where it connects to the plant. For Hybrid Teas and Grandifloras a good rule of thumb is to remove anything smaller in diameter than a pencil. For other roses, gauge by what the healthiest canes look like.

6. Prune to an open shape to encourage healthy air circulation. Look for canes that cross and take out whichever is smaller. Remove any others that look out of place. Keep the canes well spaced.

7. Make cuts in correct relation to the buds as follows: Look for outward-facing buds, or eyes, and cut at an angle ¼ to ⅛ inch above

each, so that the slope angles away from the bud at a 45° angle. Closer cuts may injure the buds or cause them to dry up. Cuts placed too far above the bud cause the cane to die back.

8. Place cuts properly. The shape the plant takes depends on the buds you choose. In most cases you should prune above buds that point away from the interior of the bush. As they grow they will spread out into an open, attractive habit. Buds that face the center of the bush will form in that direction. This is useful for training naturally spreading roses into a more upright habit, but is otherwise just asking for crossed canes and an untidy bush.

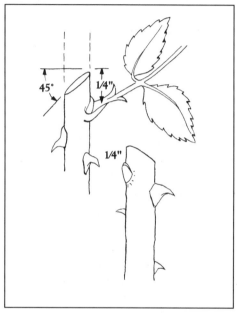

Proper relation of the pruning cut to a leaf (with bud eye) and to a bud.

9. Pull root suckers on grafted roses. Hybrid Teas and others that are grafted onto rootstocks may occasionally send up suckers from the roots that will steal strength from the flowering variety. This is most common when the rose has been planted too deeply. The suckers should be removed whenever noticed by digging down and snapping them from their point of origin. Cutting them off at ground level only encourages more shoots.

10. Remove spent flowers. This is called dead-heading. It encourages further bloom and prevents decaying petals from introducing disease. The blossoms should not be simply picked from the stems, but instead pruned down to a healthy five-leaflet leaf. The stem will continue to grow in the direction the bud beneath the last leaf is pointed, so choose these leaves as in rule 8.

A Harvest Soft and Sweet

Roses are the glory of any garden, but their talents do not end at the garden gate. The beauty of a rose can sway the heart. The errant lover seeks forgiveness by first offering a rose, or perhaps an armload of them. Brides carry them in bouquets. Nothing can challenge the elegance of roses as a centerpiece—whether in a grand arrangement or as a single rosebud in a slender vase. Cutting your own roses for such auspicious ends is a fulfilling experience when approached with care.

When cutting roses your objective is twofold: beautiful flowers and a bush that can recover quickly. When cutting from young plants, take a minimum of stem and leave as much foliage as possible to feed the plant. Reserve the long-stemmed cuttings for established bushes over three years old.

Cutting is actually a form of summer pruning, with similar results. Place the cut so that at least two leaves remain on the shoot. Look for healthy three- to seven-leaflet leaves. New growth will sprout from the bud just beneath the last remaining leaf.

For the Perfect Bouquet of Roses:

- Harvest at dusk or dawn, in the cool of the day.

- Carry a container of water as you harvest and put each rose in water up to the bloom as soon as it is cut.

- Do not cut fully opened blossoms. They won't last. Instead, cut a variety of blossom stages, from buds to half-open flowers, for an appealing natural look.

- Allow cut blossoms to rest in water in a cool, dark place such as the refrigerator before arranging. Remove any leaves and thorns that will be below water level. Never scrape them, as this injures the stem. Break them off with your fingers or wrap a dishcloth around the neck of the blossom and gently pull downward.

- When ready to arrange, make a fresh, slanted cut ½ inch above the original and scrape the bark from the bottom ½ inch of the remaining stem.

- Place the fresh cut immediately in hot (120°F) water. After the water cools, place the whole works in the refrigerator. This hot–cold therapy conditions the blooms and revives wilting bouquets.

- Arrange the roses in fresh water. Add a floral preservative or some clear, non-diet citrus soda pop (Sprite, 7-Up, etc.) to extend the life of the blossoms.

- Freshen or replace the water daily and make a fresh cut at the base of each stem.

- Keep the arrangement in a cool, draft-free spot, out of direct sunlight.

Now that you have mastered tending your roses, including pruning and harvesting to bring their beauty and fragrance indoors, there is one more consideration. The next chapter looks at ways of incorporating the "Queen of Flowers" into your landscape plans.

CHAPTER 10

North Coast Rosescaping

Whether you design your landscape around roses or work them into an existing landscape, few plants are more versatile. With hundreds of variations in flower color, bloom time, growth habit, and form, there is a rose for any landscape need.

CONSIDER THE POSSIBILITIES

Roses will work for you from the ground up. Choose a low-growing, spreading variety such as 'Champlain' or 'Charles Albanel' (both red) or the white *Rosa × paulii* over an unsightly patch of ground. Line a walkway or border with Miniatures or short-statured Floribundas. An Old Garden Rose can be a focal point in the garden or an elegant back-drop. A row of Shrub Roses will serve as a thorny hedge to enforce your property lines with style. Vigorous Climbers can create a privacy screen, frame an entryway, or transform a forlorn shed into a thing of beauty.

Take a look at several area gardens to get ideas. In one driveway near my house are lines of red-blooming 'Europeana', a Floribunda, fronted with smoky dusty miller. Down the street, an orange-blooming Tree Rose is surrounded by a ring of five yellow Floribundas that, in turn, are fronted by apricot Miniatures. Farther down the street, you can smell the Sweetbriar (*Rosa eglanteria*) hedge before you see it and the mass of perennials flowing from its wake. Trumpet-shaped daylilies herald the bouncy blossoms of shrub roses; ornamental grasses and herbs blend together in a carpet of textured green beneath the blooms. Finally, at the end of the street, a drop-off is shaded by an immense maple draped in a wave of constantly blooming 'Scarlet Meidiland'.

In Victorian times, the fashion was to segregate the garden into sections. The tradition has held with roses, partly because of the increased efficiency in performing routine gardening chores. It is more convenient to tend the garden when the plants are all in one area.

However, as long as the sites you choose meet the rose's requirements for sunlight, drainage, and air circulation, roses can be worked into the yard at will. You may have to walk a few more steps at pruning time, but a yard full of roses is worth a little exercise.

A Formal Rose Garden

Not just for parks and manors, a formal rose garden also can be yours. The overall image is one of symmetry and balance, both in color and form. Design is the key. Achieve the formal look through straight lines or precise curves. Use healthy, close-cropped turf as a foundation for a formal display, the lush green complementing the colorful blossoms. The rose beds will break up the turf in geometric shapes of intricate patterns. Set the tone for elegance with an entryway, framed by climbing roses draped over an arch or guarded by a pair of rose-tree sentries.

Get the most from a formal design by incorporating a special focal point. This could be as simple as a rose-framed bench, or as elaborate as a full-sized gazebo. Or frame the garden through a window so that you can enjoy it from inside your home, as well as from outside. Picture a wooden or stone deck for entertaining—surrounded by lovely, lavish roses.

An Informal Approach

If exact lines and strict design do not fit your garden plan, remember that nothing goes casual better than roses. They sprawl, crawl, climb, and stand up. Fit in a rose wherever you want a splash of color or a fragrant focal point.

Plan an informal rose garden more loosely than the formal kind, though landscape designer Jane Garrison incorporates straight lines to avoid a cluttered look. "The clean lines established by straight rows create a more peaceful, less busy look," she says. She points out that the simplicity of designing ornamental beds in straight lines is especially suited to very small, urban plots.

A Cutting Garden

If you long for bouquets of roses to grace your table or to perfume your home, set aside an area as a cutting garden. Although it certainly can be planned to please the eye, the primary purpose is to provide cut flowers.

Exhibition roses, public or private, are treated differently than landscape roses. They are pruned back hard in the spring to produce fewer, more spectacular blooms. The bushes are often not all that attractive on their own but can be played up with creative companion planting. Use low-growing Minis or Floribundas to skirt the edges of the cutting garden and to provide a pleasing face of foliage and color.

Training and Pegging

Two intriguing ways to show off your roses involve training Climbers or Ramblers and pegging trailing varieties.

USING CLIMBERS AND RAMBLERS Climbing varieties can be trained to follow a pre-determined course. These are vigorous varieties that send out long shoots every year. Ramblers, such as 'American Pillar', do well trained vertically on a post or trellis. Others perform their best when trained horizontally along a fence or wall. Some only bloom near the end of the shoots when trained upright, while horizontal training will spur the growth of flowering side shoots in most varieties.

Training is easy. First, choose a trellis or support appropriate to the potential size of the rose. Ramblers are very vigorous growers and must have a very sturdy support, such as grand porch posts or a big old tree. Large-Flowered Climbers and climbing Hybrid Teas are most versatile and can be trained along trellises, fences, and heavy wire strung between posts. Be sure to space trellises at least 6 inches from any walls or solid structures to allow for adequate air circulation.

During the first two years of training, let the rose grow as it wishes. In the spring of its third year, gently tie the canes in place with a soft cord or strips of cloth. As the canes grow and produce side shoots, tie them in place. The original canes will thicken over time to form a trunk-like stem. From then on, only the new canes need to be trained.

The design firm of Withey-Price delights in climbing roses and the flowing forms they can create with them. "We have espaliered 'Alchymist'," relates Glenn Withey. "It does best when cut back severely. We trained 'Sombreuil' up a holly hedge, which worked quite well, and a yellow Climber into a black elderberry bush."

PEGGING FOR EFFECT For a dramatic flair, try pegging. The best candidates are varieties that send out flexible canes from 5 to 8 feet long, such as many Bourbons and Hybrid Perpetuals. 'Félicité Parmentier' and 'Madame Pierre Oger' respond enthusiastically to this training, as does the white shrub 'Nevada', which can be pegged to stunning effect. The process isn't difficult but it does demand nearly constant attention, as new canes are constantly popping up.

Pegging cannot begin until the canes have grown for a couple of months. Trying to bend and force immature canes will only break them. Hold down canes with pegs made from 10-inch pieces of heavy, stiff wire, old clothes hangers, or metal hooks (about 8 inches long). Catch the end of a cane in the hook of a peg and anchor it into the soil. Pull the canes out flat into a circle, arch them into a low mound, swirl them, or peg them into any configuration that radiates from the center.

Turning Fences into Paradise

When a branch of the YWCA consulted Jane Garrison on a sensitive problem, she was happy to provide a rosy answer.

"They needed the security of a fence," Garrison recalls, "but at the same time that would have been very harsh looking. Instead we went with a hedge of Rugosa Roses. It looks and smells wonderful and it got the same job done that the fence would have."

Unlike many landscapers, Garrison is partial to using roses, even though her early training in the maritime Northwest discouraged their use in favor of evergreens. Her preference is to work with Rugosas and Shrub Roses for the combined effect of flowers and foliage. She especially likes the variety 'Pink Meidiland' as a hedge rose, a single-blooming, vigorous-growing variety.

Jean Rogers has a huge laurel hedge at one end of her garden. The scale might have intimidated a less creative gardener, but she planted a shorter hedge of old-fashioned varieties along one side of the laurel, allowing her to enjoy both plants.

A hedge of roses is one way to enjoy a mass planting of roses in a restricted space, all the while serving a functional purpose. A row of 'Bonica', 'Sevilliana', 'Pink Meidiland', 'Felicia', or 'Sexy Rexy', among numerous others, makes a pretty, tough boundary line.

Working with Other Plants

Other plants—perennials, annuals, shrubs, and so forth—can be included to complement your color scheme and to give a richer texture to the visual "feel." Fringe the rose beds with bright blue lobelia for eye-catching contrast. Bright yellow marigolds, frilly sweet alyssum, or small flowering herbs can be worked in and among the roses. Just be sure you provide ample water.

Many landscapers feel that roses should not be set apart in the landscape but rather woven into the overall fabric of an integrated design. Dan Hinkley prefers to see roses planted among perennials. "I don't like a formal rose garden look," he says. Rather than rows, lines, or hedges, he interplants with other blooming plants, using low-growing perennials such as ornamental grasses, dianthus, and oregano to mask bare bases.

Any corner of the yard can be transformed into a luxurious rose border or mixed border. Begin with low-growing violets, sedum, or herbs in the front of the border. If the border or parts of it are within retaining walls, let cascades of sweet alyssum or lobelia drape over the retaining wall of the bed. Next, move up to taller growing plants such as dusty miller, achillea, sweet woodruff, or *Clematis viticella*. Tuck a plush Floribunda such as 'Sexy Rexy', whose sprays can produce up to 50 blooms each, into the foreground and position two or three Hybrid Teas behind it. Other plants, such as aruncus (goat's beard) or yarrow, provide contrasting color and form. Large Shrub Roses or a trellised Climber can be intermingled with other climbing vines such as a restrained variety of honeysuckle or trumpet vine, to provide a dramatic backdrop.

Dan Borroff frequently uses the drought-tolerant *Rosa glauca* as a backdrop to perennials. He recommends choosing pink- to purple-blooming flowers to complement the foliage. This is also a popular choice with Withey-Price, for both its unique foliage and its fall display of hips; they generally prefer working with Species, threading them into intricate patterns with other plants. "We like to grow them with clematis such as 'Viticella', 'Lady Betty Belfore', and 'Florida'. When the rose is spent, the clematis takes over," explains Charles Price.

A birdbath in the garden adds a third dimension to the pleasures therein, the melodies of bird song. Remember that inviting birds into the garden encourages natural pest control: those that come to bathe may stay to dine. Take the idea a step further by including a garden fountain. The sound of running water will attract birds and soothe you.

MAKING THE ROSE BED

Whether you carve out an elaborate formal design or squeeze in an odd grouping here and there, roses are usually planted in beds.

Consider height and form in your design plan. Place short-growing or less vigorous roses toward the south end of the planting so those in the background will receive more sunlight than if they were shaded by taller varieties. Use differences in height to create a constant flow of foliage and flowers from the ground up. Minis and low-growing Floribundas can be used in the foreground, and to help "cover the ankles" of roses that tend to be somewhat bare at the base. Place Hybrid Teas and Grandifloras behind the shorter varieties and use taller growing varieties or Climbers to provide a lush backdrop.

Most modern roses, when planted in groups, make the nicest display when the sides of neighboring bushes just touch. Crowding cheats the individual plants and impairs their growth, while sparse planting looks stingy. Plant double, alternating rows, an attractive method for positioning roses in beds that allows plants to receive maximum sun as well as root space.

When planting roses en masse, try to keep the overall look uncluttered. Too many different colors planted together can be distracting to the eye, cautions Charles Price. "It looks best to color coordinate the blossoms," he advises. "If you want to chase the rainbow, blend the colors so that they merge through. If you start with yellow bloomers, ease into coral, then orange, and on to reds, for instance. Also avoid putting colors that detract from one another too close together."

Give the roses enough elbow room around heavy feeders or large-rooted plants such as shrubs and trees. Trees that can share diseases should not be planted nearby; keep roses 20 feet away from them.

There are many ways to extend the season of the rose. Incorporate varieties such as 'Geranium' or Rugosas known for their fall displays of bright hips. Work in those with bright fall foliage, stems, or thorns. Try your hand at preserving those heady fragrances by making potpourris. Dried roses make lovely additions to dried flower arrangements or wreaths. Rose petals also can be made into liquor or jelly or included in recipes for their unusual flavor. Once you begin to discover the many charms of this incomparable flower, you will find countless ways to savor the beauty and fragrance long after the last rose of summer.

Monthly Rose Care

For detailed information about rose care, refer to chapters designated in parentheses.

January: Test soil (3, 4). Prepare new planting sites (3, 4).

February: Begin pruning (9).

March: Finish pruning. Plant bare-root roses (6). Begin spray program (8).

April: Treat roses to compost or other rose food (4, 7). Weed (4, 7) and mulch (7). Continue spray program (8).

May: Patrol for insects (8). If using commercial rose food, reapply (7). Finish planting potted roses (5). Continue spray program (8).

June: Take softwood cuttings or layer new plants (5). Collect bouquets or blooms (9). If using commercial rose food, reapply (7). Continue spray program (8).

July: Be sure roses receive sufficient water (6, 7). Prune once-flowering varieties after blooming is finished (9). Continue spray program (8).

August: Patrol for mites (8). Discontinue commercial rose food by midmonth. Dead-head bushes (9) and gather and burn fallen leaves. Continue spray program (8).

September: Check for pests (8). Continue spray program (8).

October: Leave spent blossoms to induce dormancy (7). Discontinue watering. Continue spray program (8).

November: Cut back wind-threatened growth (9). Clean up all dropped foliage, strip leaves, and, if necessary, put up winter protection (3, 6, 7, 9). Discontinue spray program.

December: Apply dormant oil sprays (8). Start dreaming over rose catalogs (see "Rose Buying Directory," page 88).

Rose Buying Directory

COTTAGE CREEK NURSERY: 13232 Avondale Road, Woodinville, WA 98072; (206) 883-8252. *No shipping; can't reply to out-of-state correspondence.*

EDMUNDS' ROSES: 6235 SW Kahle Road, Wilsonville, OR 97070; (503) 682-1476. *Ships November to May.*

GREENMANTLE NURSERY: 3010 Ettersburg Road, Garberville, CA 95440; (707) 986-7504. *Ships January through March; list available for stamped legal-sized envelope.*

HEIRLOOM OLD GARDEN ROSES: 24062 NE Riverside Drive, St. Paul, OR 97137; (503) 538-1756. *Ships year-round in pots.*

HERONSWOOD NURSERY: 7530 288th NE, Kingston, WA 98346; (206) 297-4172. *Visits by appointment; catalog, $3.*

JACKSON & PERKINS CO.: One Rose Lane, Medford, OR 97501-0702; (800) 292-4769. *Mail order and nursery.*

JUSTICE MINIATURE ROSES: 5947 Kahle Road, Wilsonville, OR 97070; (503) 682-2370. *Retail.*

MOLBAK'S GREENHOUSE AND NURSERY: 13625 NE 175th, Woodinville, WA 98072; (206) 483-5000. *Retail.*

THE OLD ROSE GARDEN: 17908 80th Avenue NE, Bothell, WA 98011; (206) 483-4533. *Retail, no shipping.*

OREGON MINIATURE ROSES, INC.: 8285 SW 185th Avenue, Beaverton, OR 97007-5742; (503) 649-4482. *Retail, free color catalog.*

PICKERING NURSERIES, INC.: 670 Kingston Road, Highway 2, Pickering, Ont. L1V 1A6, Canada; (416) 839-2111. *Sells nonpatented only to U.S.; catalog, $3.*

RAINTREE NURSERY: 391 Butts Road, Morton, WA 98356; (206) 496-6400. *Mail order.*

ROSE FARM: 26746 13th Avenue, Aldergrove, B.C. VOX 1A0, Canada; (604) 856-2631. *Bare-root roses available late October to December, February to March; potted roses, April to June. No shipping.*

ROSES OF YESTERDAY & TODAY: 802 Brown's Valley Road, Watsonville, CA 95076; (408) 724-3537. *Ships January to May; catalog, $3.*

WAYSIDE GARDENS: #1 Garden Lane, Hodges, SC 29695-0001; (800) 845-1124. *Mail order.*

WELLS MEDINA NURSERY: 8300 NE 24th. Bellevue, WA 98004; (206) 454-1853. *Retail.*

For international orders:

(Before ordering, request import permit forms from Permit Unit, USDA, PPQ, Federal Building, Room 638, Hyattsville, MD 20782. Submit order tags with each order.)

DAVID AUSTIN ROSES: Bowling Green Lane, Albrighton, near Wolverhampton, WV7 3HB, England.

PETER BEALES ROSES: London Road, Attleborough, Norfolk NR17 1AY, England.

R. HARKNESS & CO. LTD.: The Rose Gardens, Cambridge Road, Hitchin, Hertfordshire, SG4 0JT, England.

W. KORDES SÖHNE, 2206 Klein Offenseth, Sparrieshoop, Germany.

Sources

Northwest Soil-Testing Facilities

OREGON STATE UNIVERSITY: Soil Testing Laboratory, Strand Agricultural Hall #114, Corvallis, OR 97331; (503) 754-2187.

COFFEY LAB, INC.: 4914 NE 120th Avenue, Portland, OR 98230; (503) 254-1794.

PROVINCIAL SOIL TEST LAB: B.C. Ministry of Agriculture, 1873 Spall Street, Kelowna, B.C. V1Y 4R2, Canada.

Societies and Advice

THE AMERICAN ROSE SOCIETY (ARS): PO Box 30,000, Shreveport, LA 71130; (318) 938-5402. *The ARS will refer you to your local ARS group. Membership and publications are invaluable.* Members receive 11 issues of The American Rose Magazine *plus the* American Rose Annual *(with information on rose performance),* The Handbook for Selecting Roses *(with ARS ratings), and options to buy smaller bulletins on specific topics.*

PACIFIC NORTHWEST DIRECTORY (FOR OREGON, WASHINGTON, BRITISH COLUMBIA, ALASKA, AND PART OF MONTANA): Wayne Covington, 2100 Third Avenue #2403, Seattle, WA 98121; (206) 728-5856. $3 postpaid. *Lists consulting rosarians, accredited horticultural judges, accredited rose arrangement judges, rose societies (meetings, officers, shows).*

DISTRICT DIRECTORY FOR NORTHERN CALIFORNIA, NEVADA, AND HAWAII: Rose Gilardi, 1438 26th Avenue, San Francisco, CA 94122. (415) 665-5132. *For members, $2. Lists consulting rosarians, accredited horticultural judges, accredited rose arrangement judges, rose societies (meetings, officers, shows), programs, and gardens.*

HERITAGE ROSES GROUP (NORTHWEST REGION): Judi Dexter, 23665 41st Avenue S., Kent, WA 98032.

Bibliography

American Rose Society. THE HANDBOOK FOR SELECTING ROSES: A ROSE BUYING GUIDE FROM THE AMERICAN ROSE SOCIETY. Shreveport, LA: ARS, 1993

Dobson, Beverly R. COMBINED ROSE LIST. All roses currently in commerce and how to find them. c/o Peter Schneider, PO Box 16035, Rocky River, OH 44116.

Hart, Rhonda M. BUGS, SLUGS, AND OTHER THUGS: CONTROLLING GARDEN PESTS ORGANICALLY. Pownal, VT: Garden Way Publishing, 1991.

Lovejoy, Ann. THE YEAR IN BLOOM. Seattle: Sasquatch Books, 1987.

Mechlin, Stuart, and Ellen Bonanno. WITHOUT A THORN. Portland, OR: Timber Press, 1978.

Ortho Books. ALL ABOUT ROSES. San Ramon, CA: Chevron Chemical Company, 1990.

Osborne, Robert. HARDY ROSES. Pownal, VT: Garden Way Publishing, 1991.

Phillips, Roger, and Martyn Rix. ROSES. New York: Random House, 1988.

Sunset Books. ROSES. Menlo Park, CA: Sunset Publishing Corporation, 1989.

Young, Norman. THE COMPLETE ROSARIAN. New York: St. Martin's Press, 1971.

Whitner, Jan Kowalczewski. GARDEN TOURING IN THE PACIFIC NORTHWEST: A GUIDE TO GARDENS AND SPECIALTY NURSERIES IN OREGON, WASHINGTON, AND BRITISH COLUMBIA. Edmonds, WA: Alaska Northwest Books, 1993.

More Reading

For a selected list of the most current books on roses (compiled by Valerie Easton, librarian, Elisabeth C. Miller Library of the University of Washington Center for Urban Horticulture), send a stamped, self-addressed #10 envelope to: Cascadia Gardening Series, Sasquatch Books, 1931 Second Avenue, Seattle, WA 98101.

Public Gardens

These inspiring rose gardens were suggested by garden travel writer Jan Kowalczewski Whitner.

British Columbia

Richmond: Fantasy Garden World
Rosedale: Minter Gardens
Vancouver: Stanley Park Rose Garden and Queen Elizabeth Park
Victoria: Butchart Gardens and Government House Gardens

California

Berkeley: Berkeley Municipal Rose Garden
San Jose: San Jose Municipal Public Gardens

Oregon

Corvallis: Corvallis Rose Garden
Eugene: George E. Owen Memorial Rose Garden
Medford: Jackson & Perkins Test and Display Garden
Portland: The International Rose Test Garden in Washington Park
    and the Sunken Rose Garden at Peninsula Park
Salem: Bushes Pasture Park and Deepwood Gardens

Washington

Bellingham: Fairhaven Park Rose Garden
Carnation: Carnation Research Farm grounds
Olympia: Washington State Capitol grounds
Port Townsend: Rothschild House
Seattle: Woodland Park Rose Garden
Tacoma: Lakewold and the Point Defiance Park Rose Garden

Index of Common Rose Names

General Index

(Page numbers in bold type indicate material found in tables and illustrations.)